P9-BYY-694

# JET
## WARBIRDS

N611JR

WB188

## Michael O'Leary

Motorbooks International
Publishers & Wholesalers

*To the memory of Dave Zeuschel*

First published in 1990 by Motorbooks International Publishers & Wholesalers, P O Box 2, 729 Prospect Avenue, Osceola, WI 54020 USA

© Michael O'Leary, 1990

All rights reserved. With the exception of quoting brief passages for the purposes of review no part of this publication may be reproduced without prior written permission from the publisher

Motorbooks International is a certified trademark, registered with the United States Patent Office

The information in this book is true and complete to the best of our knowledge. All recommendations are made without any guarantee on the part of the author or publisher, who also disclaim any liability incurred in connection with the use of this data or specific details

We recognize that some words, model names and designations, for example, mentioned herein are the property of the trademark holder. We use them for identification purposes only. This is not an official publication

Motorbooks International books are also available at discounts in bulk quantity for industrial or sales-promotional use. For details write to Special Sales Manager at the Publisher's address

Library of Congress Cataloging-in-Publication Data
O'Leary, Michael (Michael D.)
    Jet warbirds / Michael O'Leary.
      p.  cm.
    ISBN 0-87938-476-X
    1. Jet planes, Military.  2. Jet planes, Military—Conservation and restoration.
    I. Title.
UG1240.O43  1990       90-33858
358.4'183—dc20        CIP

Printed and bound in Hong Kong

**On the frontispiece:** *Comfortable with very close formation flying, Robb Satterfield positions de Havilland Venom N502DM for a close look at the photographer. Operational Venoms were equipped with four 20 mm cannon, fortunately absent in the jet warbird variant.*

**On the title page:** *NASA test pilot Ed Schneider is seen piloting the Combat Jets Flying Museum's Hawker Hunter Mk. 51. Painted overall scarlet and carrying the RAF serial WB188, the aircraft honors the record-breaking prototype Hunter which set* an absolute world speed record of 727.6 mph on 7 September 1953 while being flown by Neville Duke.

**On this page:** *Over the small town of Mojave, which is used to unusual jet activity, the Northrop Talon leads two US Navy QF-86F drones for a bit of tail chasing.*

# Contents

# Acknowledgments

In an undertaking of this size, many people assist in the completion of the final product. I have listed essential personnel by chapter, people without whom I could not have completed this book. I would first like to thank Editor Greg Field and Publisher Tim Parker for making the whole project possible.

Gloster Meteor: Al Hansen, Ascher Ward and Skip Holm. The camera platform was a Beech Bonanza with Jeff Kertes piloting.

De Havilland Vampire and Venom: Pete Regina, Alan Preston, Dean Martin, Gene Fisher, Ascher Ward and Skip Holm. Camera platforms included a Piper Seneca flown by Bruce Guberman, a P-51D Mustang flown by Dave Zeuschel, a P-51B flown by Pete Regina and a T-28 Fennec flown by Bruce Guberman.

Lockheed Shooting Star: Ray Maybrey; Rick and Anne Brickert; Frank, Dennis, Brian and Ruth Sanders; Dick Martin; Neil Anderson; Howard Pardue; Matt Jackson; Pascal Mahvi; and Dave Zeuschel. Camera platforms included a T-6 Texan flown by Bruce Guberman, a B-25 Mitchell flown by Bruce Guberman and Jeff Kertes, a B-25 Mitchell flown by Steve Hinton, a Piper Seneca flown by Bob McKinnon and a P-51B Mustang flown by Pete Regina.

Grumman Panther: Jack Levine, Arthur Wolk and Alan Preston. Camera platforms included Alan Preston's MS.760 Paris and a Beech AT-11 Kansan flown by Clair Potter.

Mikoyan-Gurevich MiGs: Norman Suits, Bruce Goessling, Al Redick, Morgan Merrill, Jim Robinson and Paul "Geraldo" Entrekin. Camera platforms included an SF.260 flown by Brian Sanders and a Lockheed T-33 flown by Steve Gage.

North American Sabre: Dave and Annette Zeuschel, Pete Regina, Jim Robinson, Chuck Scott, Leroy Penhall, Flight Systems, Paul Metz, Dick Wright, Steve Hinton and Skip Holm. Camera platforms included a P-51D flown by Dave Zeuschel, a P-51D flown by Angelo Regina, a P-51B flown by Pete Regina, a B-25 flown by Bruce Guberman and Jeff Kertes, a T-33 flown by Steve Gage and a Beech Bonanza flown by Jeff Kertes.

Fouga Magister: Dean Martin, Tony Ritzman, Aero Trader, James Oliver and John Silberman. Camera platforms included a B-25 flown by Bruce Guberman and Jeff Kertes, a Beech Bonanza flown by Bruce Guberman and a Piper Saratoga flown by Bruce Guberman.

Hawker Hunter: Al Letcher, Al Hansen, Ascher Ward, Jim Robinson, Spencer Flack, Dave Straight and Ed Schneider. The camera platform was a T-33A flown by Steve Gage.

Douglas Skyhawk: Guy Neeley, Pascal Mahvi, Bruce Goessling and Flight Systems. The camera platform was a B-25 Mitchell flown by Bruce Guberman and Jeff Kertes.

Saab Draken: Skip Holm, Bill Marizan and Al Hansen. Camera plane was a P-51D flown by Matt Jackson.

Temco Pinto: Mike Dillon, Steve Dillon and Rick Brickert. Camera plane was a Beech T-34 Mentor flown by Steve Dillon.

Northrop Talon: Chuck Thornton, Dave Zeuschel and Skip Holm. Camera platforms included a Beech Bonanza flown by Bruce Guberman and a B-25 Mitchell flown by Bruce Guberman and Jeff Kertes.

A special thank you for Jim Robinson, Chuck Parnell and all the members of the Classic Jet Aircraft Association.

Virtually all the photographs in this volume were taken with Nikon cameras and lenses. Kodachrome 25 and 64 captured all the images.

*Paul Metz test flies QF-86F 808 (the 108th Sabre drone conversion by the NSI Division of Mantech. Northrop had previously done the conversions but sold the division to Mantech in 1988).*

# Chapter 1

# Back to the future

Aviation, for the most part, is an individualist's pursuit. It is, of course, divided into many factions but perhaps the most individualistic of any of these is the one known as warbirds. By way of definition, the term "warbird" usually applies to former military aircraft that operated or were designed during World War II. Warbird currently does not mean just fighter or bomber aircraft—the term also encompasses trainer, liaison and transport aircraft.

Basically, the modern warbird movement started in the late 1960s when restored former military aircraft began flying in their original combat colors. Until that time, the pilot who purchased a military surplus aircraft was considered downright strange. In fact, many airfields during the 1950s would not allow operations by former military fighter planes. The pilots who owned these planes, usually purchased for just a couple thousand dollars, had to seek fields that were friendly to their type of aircraft.

When the warbird movement started, such aircraft quickly became popular for airshow work and organizers of aerial events suddenly found it wise to include as many of these veter-

*The American government was extremely efficient in scrapping the USAF's and Navy's first- and second-generation jet warplanes. This North American F-86H Sabre, last assigned to the Massachusetts Air National Guard, is seen awaiting the chop at Davis-Monthan AFB during June 1967. The few H model Sabres that did survive were assigned to the Navy, which destroyed them as target drones.*

an and vintage aircraft as possible, for the public loved the sight and sound of warbirds. Organizations such as the Confederate Air Force and the Planes of Fame Air Museum did much in the early development of the warbird movement to preserve and restore World War II aircraft to their former glory. It was not an easy task; the Federal Aviation Administration (FAA) has never been overly friendly to this type of aircraft—or the owners, parts and airframes have always been difficult to find, and, as the movement continued and popularized, prices have risen to astronomical levels.

It is rather depressing for the aviation enthusiast to realize that only about one out of a thousand World War II aircraft survive—and that is for the more popular aircraft types like the P-51 Mustang. For some other types, the surviving—much less flying—number is considerably less. Messerschmitt 109s, Focke-Wulf 190s and Mitsubishi Zeros are nearly extinct, and that is a sad fact considering over 30,000 Me 109s were built!

As the warbird movement thrived, it became obvious that the number of airframes available for purchase or restoration was finite. At that point, other former military aircraft were included under the term of warbird, machines such as the Beech T-34 Mentor and the North American T-28 Trojan. Also, former military aircraft from conflicts other than World War II entered the group. Air warriors like the rugged Douglas Skyraider (which saw service in Korea and Vietnam) are now warbirds in the truest sense. With the horror of Vietnam beginning to recede, Cessna O-1 and O-2 FACs (forward air control) became popular airshow display craft.

These warbirds have one thing in common: They are all powered by reciprocating engines with propellers. It wasn't until the late 1970s that a new category began to emerge in the vintage and veteran aircraft movement: the jet warbird.

It seems that the governments of all nations have one common thread: They are all very efficient when it comes to the scrapping of military aircraft. The United States took the idea of "beating swords into plowshares" to heart and the mightiest air armada ever constructed was reduced to scrap just a few years after the victorious conclusion of World War II. Actually, it's almost pure luck that the few flying aircraft we have today survived.

Elsewhere the same was true. The war-weary British destroyed vast fleets of Spitfires, Hurricanes and Lancasters. The aircraft belonging to the defeated nations were blown up in mass quantities to ensure against any possible future, hostile use. A few military aircraft were parceled off as surplus to friendly nations and these planes served to later bolster the ranks of the warbird movement.

The huge jet fleets constructed by Britain, United States and France during the late 1940s and 1950s bolstered the defensive power of the Free World while expanding the technology of modern aerodynamics. It seemed that, during this time, new fighters and bombers were appearing on an almost monthly schedule. Jet aerodynamics made giant leaps and, as this happened, many aircraft quickly became obsolete and were withdrawn from service and, in the majority of instances, simply scrapped. The US Navy stored its planes at NAS Litchfield Park,

*Stripped of parts, an RAF Hawker Hunter is prepared for scrapping. This most attractive of all British jet fighters still flies operationally with several air forces.*

*Britain was as efficient as the United States when it came to scrapping jet aircraft. This well-weathered Gloster NF.14 Meteor night fighter awaits the axe at a British field during the 1960s.*

while the USAF used nearby Davis-Monthan AFB, both in Arizona. Vast fleets of planes kept at these facilities and were usually stripped of parts that had application in other areas and then sold to civilian scrappers.

These facilities were combined in the early 1960s at Davis-Monthan AFB into what was dubbed the "desert air force." Early jets were quickly melted down for valuable aluminum. A few were passed on to foreign air arms, but the majority of planes were simply terminated with prejudice. A photo printed in the popular press depicting a virtual mountain of scrapped F–84 Thunderjets caused a public outcry about where defense dollars were going and even caused Davis-Monthan to be temporarily closed off from the "prying" eyes of the press! Thus, during this period, we lost the majority of

our first- and second-generation jet warplanes.

There were few individuals interested in obtaining former military jets. The government did not want to have civilians flying about in them, the FAA certainly did not want private ownership of such airplanes, but a few pilots *did* decide they wanted to own and operate high-performance jet aircraft.

In the late 1950s, an outfit called Fliteways located in West Bend, Wisconsin, made a deal to purchase several dozen surplus de Havilland Vampire Mk. 3 fighters from the Royal Canadian Air Force. The aircraft were obsolete to the Canadians and they were happy to get rid of the Vampires for a few hundred dollars each.

Fliteways began to advertise the Vampires for sale in various American aeronautical journals and, somewhat surprisingly, orders began to come in. The Vampires were sold in basically stock condition, minus weapons and a few other military items. For a couple thousand dollars a Cessna/Piper pilot could have a high-performance jet with which to impress his friends.

Licensed in the experimental category, the civilian Vampires caused the FAA to "go ballistic" and in a short time the FAA came up with dozens of reasons why civilians should not be cruising around the airways in these jets. The Vampire movement died a fairly quick death and the civil-registered examples could be seen slowly moldering into the ground at airports across the country—the planes were unsaleable because of the FAA ban.

Fliteways quickly regrouped and sold the remaining stock of Vampires to the Mexican Air Force, thus forming that nation's first jet squadron. (The FAA had another fit when the fleet of Mexican Vampires was ferried south by civilians and stopped for refueling on the way.) The first stage of the jet warbird movement was dead.

During the early 1970s, a few enterprising individuals figured out there was money—big money—in flight testing products that manufacturers were trying to sell to the military. The problem was that the equipment had to be tested on fairly high performance machines: jets.

Where were they to get such planes? The friendly Canadians were once again the answer. Planes like the F–86 Sabre and the T–33 Shooting Star had been withdrawn from RCAF service and placed in storage. Once again for a reasonable price a number of airframes were obtained, flown to the United States and licensed in the experimental category. Federal officials were puzzled but concluded that the usage of such aircraft for flight test research work was probably okay since the planes were usually flown from remote locations. Thus a precedent was set.

It wasn't long before a handful of individuals began obtaining Sabres and Shooting Stars from Canada for their own use. Leroy Penhall was particularly instrumental in bringing such aircraft onto the civil register, and his facility at Chino, California, began turning out beautifully finished examples of these planes for the private owner.

Disaster struck in 1973 when a civil-registered Sabre crashed into an ice cream parlor (conveniently placed near the end of the runway) at Sacramento, California, with a large loss of life. The pilot was unfamiliar with the Sabre and over-rotated on takeoff, causing the Sabre to mush down the runway without becoming airborne. The crash caused the FAA, and rightly so, to take a look at the standards for operating jet warbirds.

Still, the movement continued to gain strength with new aircraft restorations by Ben Hall, Dave Zeuschel, Jack Levine and others. Jet warbirds suddenly became a very popular item at airshows—much like their piston-powered brethren.

Through the 1970s and 1980s the jet warbird movement grew by leaps. Aircraft are being returned from overseas air forces for restoration while the phenomena of the Communist political collapse in the late 1980s and early 1990s has seen literally dozens of unusual jet warplanes released for sale to America. Former communists are now scrambling for their share of greenbacks, as evidenced by the impressive numbers of MiGs now flying or under restoration in the United States.

Jim Robinson of Houston, Texas, is one of the most enthusiastic jet warbird collectors. His Combat Jets Flying Museum includes planes from the T–33 to F–104 Starfighter (with a couple of MiGs thrown in for good measure) but, more importantly, Jim has had the foresight to create an organization of jet warbird owners and operators to professionally deal with the FAA and other government institutions to ensure a reasonable operating program. In 1989, the Classic Jet Aircraft Association was born. The CJAA holds regular meetings with the FAA and has taken steps to make sure the jet warbird community continues to operate and thrive.

Membership in the CJAA is open to pilots and operators (voting members) and to jet warbird enthusiasts and supporters (associate membership). The fact that this book is in your hands illustrates the dynamic growth of the jet warbird movement. Interested individuals are urged to contact the CJAA at 8802 Travelair, Houston, Texas 77061.

Keep the jet warbirds flying!

# Chapter 2

# Gloster Meteor

During the Battle of Britain, designers and builders on both sides frantically rushed to employ warplane improvements as more data was received from the combat squadrons. Aircraft engines became more powerful, armament became heavier and improved pilot protection was added as the fight continued. Situated in small design rooms on both sides of the Channel, certain development work was being carried on in great secrecy—work that would forever alter aviation. In those small, guarded rooms birth was being given to the jet warplane.

Aerodynamicists realized that piston engines and propellers would only go so fast before an impenetrable barrier in the sky was reached—a barrier that could only be transcended by a new type of propulsion system and a new style of airframe.

Development of the turbojet engine was going on in Britain and Germany during the late 1930s and a surprising number of advances had been made toward developing this new and exciting form of propulsion. In Britain, Frank Whittle had made tremendous strides in the creation of an operational jet. His powerplant was chosen

*This is how Gloster/Armstrong-Whitworth Meteor NF.11/TT.20 WD592 arrived at Mojave, California, during a warm June day in 1975. Unannounced and right in the middle of an unlimited air race, ferry pilot Jeff Hawke was running low on fuel and having radio problems. Note the full Royal Navy markings. The aircraft last served the RN as a target tug on the island of Malta.*

to power the Gloster E.28/39, an experimental airframe built specifically to test the new engine.

The E.28/39 was a stubby little airframe that mounted the Whittle W.1 turbojet which produced 860 lbs. of thrust on a good day. First flight was undertaken on 15 May 1941 from Cranwell and the combat jet age in Britain was born.

There were many problems to be overcome before a combat jet could be fielded and ominous intelligence reports from Germany indicated that the Luftwaffe was well on its way to creating a jet force. The lack of power and relative unreliability of the early turbojets dictated a two-jet layout and Gloster's F.9/40 (standing for fighter design nine submitted in 1940) proposal was chosen for production, with a contract for eight prototypes and twenty production machines being placed in September 1941.

The first Meteor completed (RAF serial DG202) was fitted with W.2B turbojets that had been built by Rover. These engines, however, were erratic—developing only about 1,000 lbs. thrust each—and it was felt this was not enough power for safe flight. Accordingly, the plane (which was originally to carry the name Thunderbolt but, because of the Republic P–47, this was changed to Meteor) was used for taxi tests. It fell upon the fifth prototype (DG206) to perform the first flight honors on 5 March 1943. DG206 was powered by two Halford H.1 turbojets, the ancestor of the de Havilland Goblin engine, each producing 1,500 lbs. of thrust.

The airframe of the Meteor was pretty traditional and the engines were housed in large nacelles near the fuselage. The cockpit was placed well forward for good visibility and the plane sat on tricycle landing gear. Armament consisted of four 20 mm cannon for a very heavy punch.

During the early testing, work continued unabated on the turbojets. The development of the Whittle units was transferred from Rover to Rolls-Royce and that hallowed company developed the W.2B/23 Welland of 1,700 lbs. thrust.

Interestingly, the first production Meteor Mk. I (EE210) was sent to the United States for testing in the middle of 1943 in exchange for a Bell Airacomet (America's first jet fighter—a plane that never went operational but served as a testbed for the development of an American turbojet).

The first RAF unit to receive the Meteor was No. 616 Squadron which was flying Spitfires at RAF Manston in Kent. Since there was no two-seat Meteor for dual-control training, the Spitfire pilots were merely given a copy of the pilot's manual and a briefing by the test pilot, and were then on their own to discover the jet age!

No. 616 Squadron received its first two Meteors on 12 July 1944 and by the end of the month the squadron was capable of fielding seven Meteors. At this time, London and southern England were catching the brunt of the "second" blitz as wave after wave of remotely piloted V–1 "buzz bombs" began smashing into the island from their continental launching pads.

The Meteor with its high top speed was pressed into service against Hitler's terror weapons. Since the V–1s flew a prescribed course, they did not take any form of evasive action and the Meteor pilot could either close on the enemy and blow it apart with a burst from the 20 mm cannon or attempt another more hazardous tactic.

The first mission against the buzz bombs by No. 616 was undertaken on 27 July but was immediately beset by problems with the firing of the 20 mm cannon. On 4 August, Flying Officer Dunn, using great resource and a fair amount of courage after his Meteor's guns also failed, stabilized his Meteor in formation with a V–1 at 365 mph and then gently eased in closer to the enemy. Raising a wingtip off the Meteor, Dunn managed to "tip" the V–1 off course. This immediately scrambled the craft's gyroscope, causing the weapon to plunge into a field and explode. This tactic had its own hazards since the weapon could explode when tipped, but firing with the cannon was also dangerous since the high-explosive warhead could detonate with tremendous force and damage or destroy the pursuing Meteor.

Throughout the remainder of the V–1 blitz, both tactics were used—the one chosen usually a matter of personal preference to the pilot. By the time the Germans had been driven from their launching platforms in Pas de Calais, France, No. 616 had destroyed thirteen flying bombs in the air.

When the Messerschmitt Me 262 twin-engine jet fighter made its presence known over the continent, the Meteors of No. 616 Squadron were prepared for possible combat with the enemy. During October 1944, Mustangs and Thunderbolts of the USAAF's 8th Air Force practiced air combat maneuvering with the Meteors in order to gain experience in dealing with hostile jet aircraft.

A flight of Meteors from No. 616 was dispatched to a field near Brussels, Belgium, to serve with the 2nd Tactical Air Force and to become the first Allied jet unit in Europe. The flight was soon joined by more Meteors from No. 504 Squadron and an operational sortie was undertaken on 16 April 1945. By this time, the Meteors were improved Mk. IIIs fitted with Rolls-Royce Derwent turbojets of 2,000 lbs. thrust each. A number of these aircraft were painted overall white. The rapid collapse of the Luftwaffe and the final surrender of the Third Reich did not allow for the Meteor to prove itself in aerial combats, but the type would go on to have a very lengthy operational service with the Royal Air Force and with the air forces of many foreign nations.

The basic Meteor airframe was greatly expanded and updated with a number of different variants that ranged in mission from that of day fighter, to two-seat night fighter, to dual-control trainer, to target tug and to many other specialized uses like ejection seat test beds. The Meteor T.7 became the RAF's first jet trainer while the Meteor F.8 was the RAF's major single-seat day fighter from 1950 to 1955. The Meteor FR.9 and PR.10 provided jet reconnaissance capabilities while Meteor NF.11 to NF.14 variants became the RAF's first jet night fighters.

It was not until 1951 that the RAF received its first jet night fighters, in the form of the NF.11 built under license by Armstrong-Whitworth. The NF.11 had a long nose to accommodate radar and a second seat added to the cockpit area for the radar navigator. Power was provided by two Rolls-Royce Derwent 8 turbojets of 3,600 lbs. thrust each, and armament consisted of four 20 mm cannon. The penultimate Meteor night fighter was the NF.14 with a large bubble canopy that replaced the earlier braced variant while adding a host of improvements. By 1956, the Meteor night fighters were being replaced by Gloster Javelins in Britain but the Meteors remained operational at front-line bases overseas until mid 1961.

Some NF.11s were converted to target tugs. RAF serial WD592 spent its night fighter life with Nos. 125, 141 and 264 Squadrons before being transferred to the Royal Navy where it was converted to a TT.20 target tug. In 1957, Armstrong-Whitworth was contracted to convert twenty-five NF.11s to TT.20s. All the night fighter gear and armament was stripped out of the airframes and winches and other associated target-tug gear were added. The first TT.20 was delivered to the Navy in early 1958. The aircraft were deployed to various bases where they participated in exercises with surface and air units of the Navy.

Quite a few TT.20s flew with No. 728 Squadron at Malta until that unit was disbanded on 31 May 1967. The

TT.20 enjoyed an exceptional safety record with just one aircraft lost during the type's thirteen years of service.

WD592 was utilized by No. 728 Squadron and then stored for several years. The plane was acquired by Al Letcher of Mojave, California, and a deal was set up with colorful aviation personality Jeff Hawke to ferry the vintage warrior across the Atlantic and America to its new home in the desert.

The arrival of WD592 at Mojave was something of a surprise since the plane came in during the middle of an unlimited air race—unannounced! Bearing full Royal Navy markings with distinctive yellow and black target tug stripes, the Meteor was a surprise to the American audience—the majority of whom had certainly never seen the type "in the flesh." A small civil registration of N94749 was carried on the vertical tail for the June 1975 ferry flight.

*The Meteor became a well-known landmark at Mojave and was one of the first civilian jet warbirds to operate from the field, which is now famous as a center for civilian-owned former military jets.*

Letcher, who has owned a variety of unusual aircraft over the years, proceeded to go through the Meteor and get the plane licensed for operation in the United States. Flown only occasionally, the Meteor became one of Mojave's better known landmarks. The plane actually did get some film work, becoming a "mystery fighter" for television's *Wonder Woman* series! Painted gloss white with RAF roundels, the aircraft looked quite distinctive but it deteriorated as the years passed—eventually to the point where it was not airworthy.

Purchased in 1988 by Al Hansen, another well-known collector of inter-

Next page
*The NF.11 was originally armed with four 20 mm cannon and was the Royal Air Force's first jet night fighter.*

esting aircraft, the Meteor was restored to flying condition during 1989 and made its first post-restoration flight with test pilot Skip Holm at the controls during November. Hansen has painted the aircraft in Royal Air Force markings complete with squadron insignia. In the foreseeable future N94749 will remain the only flying Meteor in the United States.

Two Meteors are in private hands in Britain and are being prepared for flight. Another two Meteors are operated in the United Kingdom by Martin Baker for ejection seat test work.

*Skip Holm flies the Meteor on its first post-restoration flight. Basically a first-generation jet aircraft, the NF.11 is primitive in a number of respects.*

20

# Chapter 3

# De Havilland Vampire and Venom

In order to create a first-generation jet fighter in a minimum amount of time with the least technical problems, de Havilland came up with a proposal that was emminently practical. The 100th design from the creative firm started by Capt. Geoffrey de Havilland, the DH.100 became a success for Britain and then went on to become a lucrative item for export to foreign air forces.

Design work for the DH.100 began in May 1942 and was keyed to Specification E.6/41 which called for the aircraft to have four 20 mm cannon (the British were much more in favor of heavy cannon armament during this time period than were their American allies), a pressurized cockpit and a Halford H.1 turbojet which was also being developed by a division of de Havilland Engines.

The employees at de Havilland had become very skilled in working with wooden structures, courtesy of the magnificent Mosquito. Accordingly, to save time and money, the DH.100 was designed to take advantage of this expertise, and the central nacelle that accommodated the pilot and engine was built up from layered wood. The remainder of the new airframe was light-alloy, stressed-skin construction.

An advantage of the Halford H.1 (later to be named Goblin) was that the engine had a single-sided centrifugal compressor, differing markedly from the Whittle turbojet designs. This

*This fearsome Vampire Mk. 3 is N6878D after a repainting by new owner Al Letcher who purchased the plane from Pete Regina in 1973.*

allowed intake air to be rammed directly into the eye of the impeller, which de Havilland engineers felt was a more efficient system. The engine allowed the airframe of the DH.100 to be fairly small, requiring only one powerplant, compared to the contemporary Meteor's two. The engine was fed by small wing root intakes and the turbojet was mounted in the rear of the central nacelle.

A twin-boom layout was chosen with the horizontal stabilizer mounted high to avoid the jet efflux. Because of the design layout and the fact the aircraft did not have a propeller, the landing gear legs were quite short and the DH.100 sat low to the ground in a rather menacing stance. The twin vertical tails were of the de Havilland trademark shape: graceful curving elliptical shapes that had been mounted on dozens of historic designs.

Geoffrey de Havilland, Jr., took the prototype aircraft aloft from the company's Hatfield factory on 20 September 1943. The plane's serial number was LZ548/G, the G meaning the plane had to be guarded at all times. At first, the aircraft was given the rather dreadful name of Spider Crab but this would soon change to the more sublime Vampire.

As with virtually all early jet designs, there were problems with the engine. The first-generation Goblin was rated at 2,700 lbs. thrust but flight testing was restricted to 9600 rpm, thus reducing thrust considerably. When the rpm restriction was lifted in early 1944, the aircraft easily went up to 530 mph—an impressive performance that

left the fastest of the piston-engine fighters in its jetwash.

Flight testing moved ahead with three prototypes (all minus pressurization to save time but two of the planes did have armament installed). The Air Ministry liked what they saw and an order was placed for 120 fighters. Since de Havilland was swamped with orders for Mosquitos and the like, the entire production order had to be subcontracted to English Electric.

As with any first-generation aircraft, changes occurred on the Vampire production line as more data was received from test aircraft. Canopies were modified, tail shapes changed and engines uprated. To increase range, always the sore point with early turbojets, 100 gallon fuel pods were installed under the outer wing panels. The first operational deliveries went to No. 247 Squadron during April 1945 and immediately after VE Day, foreign interest became increasingly evident and Vampires were soon flowing to Sweden and Switzerland.

The Vampire came along a bit too late to see action in World War II but the type would see combat in several parts of the globe during its lengthy service career.

The next production variant of the Vampire was the Mk. 3 which had greater range and a number of improvements. English Electric cranked out 117 Mk. 3s for the RAF, four for Norway and eighty-five for the Canadians—for whom the Mk. 3 would be their first jet fighter. Other variants came fast and furious, including aircraft for the Royal Navy, and a suitably modified Vampire undertook carrier

*The best of de Havilland's 1940s high-tech warbirds are shown in formation over central Florida. Warbird importer Dean Martin leads the flight in his all-black FB. Mk. 54 Venom N402DM (former Swiss Air Force J-1730, and former British civil-registration G-BLIA) while Alan Preston flies wing in his T. Mk. 35 Vampire N11924 (former Royal Australian Air Force serial number A79–618). As can be seen, the right clam shell gear door on Preston's Vampire remained in the down position.*

trials aboard the HMS *Ocean* on 3 December 1945 and led to the Royal Navy placing orders for a variety of Vampires.

Vampire production was also licensed to several countries including France, India and Australia. The Vampire filled an important need at the time it was built and the little fighter helped a number of air forces move into the jet age.

The final variant of the Vampire was also one of the most important. Like Lockheed, de Havilland realized that jet pilot training was completely lacking in the RAF (students still being taught on the tail dragger Harvard, the Commonwealth variant of the ubiqui-

tous Texan). Accordingly, the company invested their own funds to create the DH.115 Vampire Trainer. First flown on 15 November 1950, the DH.115 attracted RAF interest and funding was sought to put the dual-control, side-by-side trainer into production.

Designated Vampire T.11 in RAF service, the trainer was a success and 530 examples were built along with 274 aircraft for export. The Vampire was a de Havilland success story, eventually having a production run of 3,268 machines (2,464 were single-seaters) and serving with twenty-six air forces around the globe.

The Venom was a direct evolution from the basic Vampire. An effective,

but somewhat primitive, night fighter and fighter bomber, the Venom applied later high-performance technology to the basic Vampire configuration. With the DH.100 design, about the best engineers could hope for was an engine with about 3,000 lbs. of thrust and this put very definite limits on the airframe. With the Venom, engines could now be counted on to produce up to 5,000 lbs. thrust and de Havilland began to envision an "improved" Vampire.

Originally, de Havilland wanted to just change the wing and call the new aircraft the Vampire Mk. 8. However, so many changes took place that a new design number, DH.112, was issued along with the new name. The wing was larger, thinner and had what de Havilland described as "sweep back." Attempting to catch on to the new trend in jet designs, the de Havilland term really meant that the wing had a tapered leading edge that gave a critical Mach number about 0.84—better than the Meteor but nothing like the new American and Soviet fighters.

The first Venom, equipped with a Rolls-Royce Ghost, flew on 2 September 1949. Armament consisted of four 20 mm cannon with 150 rounds each, and the wing was stressed to carry wingtip tanks and an underwing pylon on each wing that could carry 1,000 lbs. of weapons.

*Pete Regina got the Vampire movement back on the right track with his restoration of Vampire Mk. 3 N6878D. The aircraft is seen on its first flight after restoration on 8 April 1972 (which, coincidentally, was also the author's first "professional" air-to-air session. Ah, the good old days of one primitive Pentax and two lenses!). This particular rebuild was a milestone in the rebirth of the jet warbird movement. The photograph was taken from the back seat of Dave Zeuschel's Mustang, N332.*

*Skip Holm test flying Ascher Ward's T. Mk. 35 N11921 (former RAAF A79–613) shortly after the aircraft had been sold to Alan Preston in July 1983. During this flight, Skip had one little problem—he couldn't get the gear down.*

Plans to build large numbers of Venoms in Britain and on the Continent did not come to fruition because of the availability of much more advanced American designs. The Venom did have a combat altitude of 51,000 ft. which was pretty good but its roll rate was classified as very poor.

First production aircraft were FB. Mk. 1s and 373 were built to equip about half the fighter-bomber squadrons in Germany. Some aircraft suffered wing structural failures and the pilots were warned not to exceed flight maneuvering limitations. Also, the aircraft did not have ejection seats, and the lack of an air conditioning system made the cockpit almost intolerable.

These faults were finally corrected on the Venom FB. Mk. 4 but this aircraft did not fly until 29 December 1953—at a time when the plane was decidedly long in the tooth. These aircraft also had a number of other airframe improvements and the Mk. 4 caught the eye of the Swiss Air Force which set up a consortium of Pilatus, FFW and Federal Aircraft to build under license 250 Venoms—many of which are still in service today.

The Venom also enjoyed a considerable production run as a night fighter with a two-crew cabin and large radar set. Once again, besides the RAF, these night fighters were purchased by other countries including Sweden and France (which built their own). In RAF service, the Venom soldiered on in the fighter-bomber role until 1962 before being phased out of service and scrapped.

In the mid 1950s, Fliteways of West Bend, Wisconsin, purchased thirty-nine surplus Vampire Mk. 3s from the Royal Canadian Air Force with the intent of selling the planes to private pilots in the United States. Little was done in the way of demilitarizing the aircraft except for the removal of weapons and a few other military items and the addition of civilian radios. Even though these aircraft carried bargain-basement prices, usually selling for well under $10,000, they did not attract much interest since

the warbird movement had not started and the average Cessna/Piper pilot was usually downright scared of such a machine.

However, there were a few hardy souls who thought a high-speed jet would be just the ticket and plunked their money down for a surplus Vampire with a fresh US experimental registration. A few of the planes began operating at airfields around the country—giving equal thrills to pilots and bystanders alike. One Vampire, N6878D, was obtained by John Morgan, painted overall gold and flown to air displays where the pilot was billed as Johnny Rocket!

A few Vampires were used as more or less legitimate business tools but the FAA became concerned as more of the planes showed up with

civilian licenses. After all, citizens weren't supposed to run around in high-speed former military jets, were they? In short order, the FAA clamped down on Vampire operations and by the late 1950s, most of the civil-registered Vampires were sinking into the ground at local airports.

Fliteways had the last laugh, however. In order to get rid of their remaining large stock of Vampires, the company cut a quick deal with Mexico and the Mexican Air Force suddenly had its first jet squadron. A mass ferry flight of Vampires across the States to Mexico caused the Feds to have one last fit of Vampire frenzy.

The airshow Vampire, N6878D, eventually wound up with the fabled Tallmantz Collection at Orange County, California, and was sold for a mere

*"One thing about a Venom, you always get their attention when you start the damn thing at an airshow," says Dean Martin. The Ghost is jolted into life by a blast of air from a cartridge starter which produces an interesting noise and a tell-tale plume of black smoke.*

$1,000 in the 1967 auction of vintage aircraft. Flown to Barstow, California, the plane sat unairworthy until obtained by Pete Regina in 1970. He flew the Vampire back to his home base at Van Nuys, California, and began a detailed restoration on the veteran fighter—culminating in a first post-restoration flight on 8 April 1972. In a way, this was a very important first flight since it began to herald the

27

return of former military jet fighters to the US civil register. Several other Vampire Mk. 3s began restoration around the country after Regina blazed the trail.

Another infusion of Vampires occurred in the 1970s when surplus Royal Australian Air Force two-seat Vampire trainers, T. Mk. 35s, were imported to the United States. Sold quite reasonably, these aircraft found ready buyers. Several more two-seaters were also imported from India and Ireland.

One of the two-seaters was dubbed "Mystery Jet" by a scam artist who apparently had a silver enough tongue to convince investors that a highly modified eight-seat Vampire business jet was just what the world was waiting for. After a considerable amount of money had changed hands, the federal investigators sent the scam artist to jail. The business jet Vampire never—and probably fortunately—took flight.

Pilots and restorers like Al Hansen, Chuck Parnell, Denny Sherman and others have made sure that the Vampire flies in American skies. Perhaps the most ambitious of all Vampire owners is Bill Dilley of Utah who has six two-seaters (three flying and three under rebuild) in his hangar that he calls Vampire Central.

With around sixteen Vampires flying or under restoration, this historic first-generation jet will remain flying for many years to come.

The man most responsible for bringing the Venom to American shores is Dean Martin, who runs a vintage aircraft sales business in Vermont. Martin travels the world in search of exotic former military aircraft that can be sold on the civilian market. On one of his wanderings he picked up a batch of former Swiss Air Force Venoms. After shipping the planes back to the States, Martin put them up for sale—the majority were purchased fairly quickly. "The Venom gives you great bang for the buck," said Martin. "It's got plenty of speed and plenty of range. It's a responsive plane with few dangerous characteristics."

Approximately eight Venoms are currently flying in the United States and as the Swiss prepare to phase out more, it's likely we will see more twin-boom de Havillands in American skies. "The Swiss maintain their military aircraft in great condition," states Martin. "The buyer of a surplus Venom is getting a hell of a deal." With the price of a Venom around $100,000, I agree!

*In order to get the Vampire's gear down and locked, Skip tried some aerobatics and was successful. A safe landing was made and the Vampire was then ferried from Van Nuys to Texas. The T. Mk. 35 spans 38 ft., is 34 ft. 6½ in. long, stands 6 ft. 2 in. high, and has a top speed of 538 mph at sea level. Power comes from a de Havilland Goblin 35 with 3,500 lbs. thrust.*

Next page
*"I wanted to get rid of that old, faded Swiss camouflage," said Dean Martin. "I got out my spray gun and painted the damn thing all black. Looked pretty good. Guess the rest of 'em liked it too since more of the flying Venoms now have the same color scheme." The Venom offers high speed and fairly long range, usually for a price around $100,000.*

# Chapter 4

# Lockheed Shooting Star

On 8 January 1944, the Lockheed XP–80 made its first flight and a significant milestone was achieved. Not only was the new aircraft designed and completed in record time, but the performance offered by the prototype's flight testing indicated that America had its first practical jet fighter. Since Britain was the leader in turbojets, the XP–80 utilized an early variant of the de Havilland Goblin that produced only 2,460 lbs. of thrust instead of the anticipated 3,000 lbs. But that figure was good enough to boost the XP–80's top speed over the 500 mph mark.

Lockheed's Kelly Johnson and the rest of the P–80 design team had come up with a winner and orders for a whopping 5,000 aircraft had been placed even before flight testing was completed. The USAAF felt they had an aircraft that could take on the new German jets ominously appearing in the war-torn skies over Fortress Europa. However, the war ended before the P–80 could be put into combat—even though a small force of P–80s had been sent to Italy for combat testing.

With the final victory over Japan, the orders for the P–80 were cut back to 1,217 aircraft and these were spread out over several variants, each with its own set of improvements. When the Korean War began, the F–80 (the P for pursuit was changed to F for fighter in June 1948) was ready and available for action and, fortunately, Lockheed production had been increased and more jets were available for combat. The F–80 scored the first jet-versus-jet victory in Korea and went on to establish an excellent record in the ground-attack role, even though the type was markedly inferior to the new Russian MiG–15s that began appearing in numbers.

There were quite a few accidents as pilots transitioned from aircraft like the Mustang to the F–80, which had been named the Shooting Star. The new USAF was slow to realize the need for a jet trainer. Pilots were still being trained in 600 hp T–6 Texans that were fine trainers for Mustangs but were inadequate for training pilots for the jet age. Introduction to the Shooting Star usually consisted of an instructor pilot explaining the layout of the new aircraft to the fledgling jet aviator and then letting him take it "around the patch" to get a feel for the new warplane.

Lockheed saw the stupidity of such a procedure and began to invest company funds in an aircraft that could accommodate both pilot and instructor. Lockheed test pilot Tony LeVier recalls Kelly Johnson stating, "The government needs a jet trainer. Right now they don't want it but they're going to get it, and I think they will like it."

*Ray Maybrey rolls his distinctive Canadair-built T-Bird away from the camera plane. N12418 is a Canadair Mk. 3 (RCAF serial number 21265) and was originally imported to the United States in 1974 by Leroy Penhall's Fighter Imports. N12418 was painted in a fanciful Thunderbirds-style paint scheme by Maybrey, who bills himself as "Captain Midnight" while attending airshows.*

*The classic lines of the T-Bird are well illustrated in this head-on shot of Rick Brickert flying the* Red Knight. *The Sanders Smokewinders put out a thick trail of smoke that is useful for airshow spectators, helping them appreciate every precision maneuver.*

The method in creating a jet trainer was simple: The Lockheed team took a P–80C and added a 38.6 in. plug in front of the wing and a 12 in. plug behind the wing. This gave the needed room for a second cockpit and dual controls while keeping the whole affair within a reasonable center of gravity.

Lockheed developed the plane, at first just called the Lockheed Trainer, with its own funds (about a million dollars), and it was a good gamble, as the new trainer would reap huge profits for the company.

The USAF liked what they saw and the plane was given the designation

TP–80C on 11 June 1948; changed to T–33A on 5 May 1949. Oddly, the F–80's name of Shooting Star was transferred over to the trainer which quickly gained the universally used nickname of T-Bird.

The first TP–80C flew from Lockheed's Van Nuys facility for the first time on 22 March 1948 with LeVier at the controls. The test pilot stated that the TP–80C flew just "like the F–80, only faster." The longer canopy over the two positions apparently helped smooth out the airflow and made the trainer marginally faster than the fighter.

LeVier and the TP–80C were dispatched on an extensive tour of USAF and USN bases in order to sell the type to the military. The large canopy was subjected to the pressure of high-speed flight and during one display it failed, and nearly cost LeVier's life. Demonstrating the trainer before USAF top brass, the canopy tore off during a high-speed pass but LeVier managed to recover control even though his helmet had been ripped away by the force of the airflow. The canopy was suitably modified so this would not reoccur.

The Air Force accepted the first production T-Bird in August 1948, and the initial production run was powered by the Allison J33–A–23 of 4,600 lbs. thrust. Later production batches were fitted with more powerful –A–25 (5,200 lbs.) and –A–35 (5,400 lbs.) jet engines. The T-Bird was an immediate hit with the American military and Lockheed went on to build 5,691 of them. Mitsubishi and Canadair were also licensed to build the type and the numbers increased with the output from these two factories. Foreign interest in the T-Bird was great and many aircraft were supplied overseas via MDAP (Mil-

*The raised sword is part of the* Red Knight's *colorful paint scheme. In Canada, the RCAF operated several different T-Birds as the* Red Knight *from 1958 through 1969.*

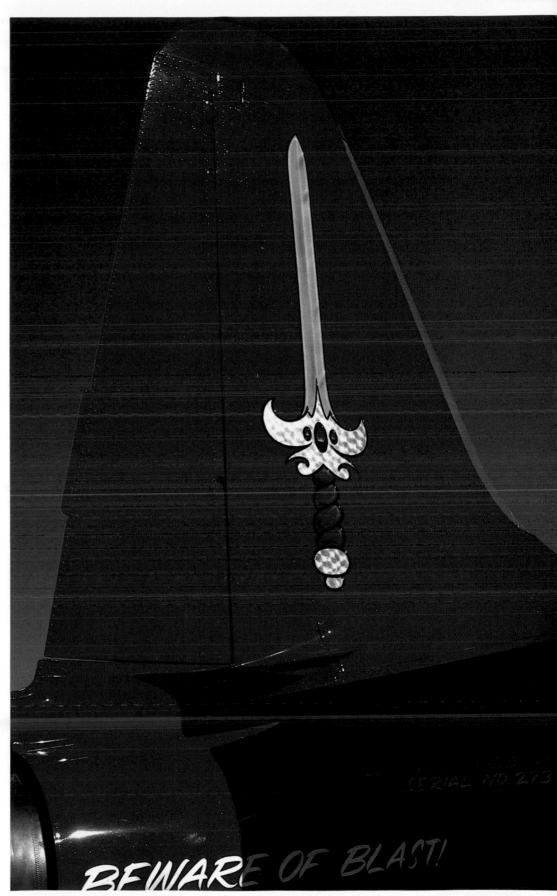

*Previous page*
*The* Red Knight *is operated by Rick Brickert and Frank and Dennis Sanders. Finished as a Royal Canadian Air Force machine, the* Red Knight *is also a Canadair-built Mk. 3 (RCAF serial number 21273) and was acquired by the* Red Knight *team in 1988 from warbird collector John Sandberg.*

itary Defense Appropriations Program) contracts.

The T-Bird became the most produced jet trainer in history and has trained more jet pilots than any other aircraft. In USAF service, the T-Bird's

*The* Red Knight *flies formation with Mike Dillon's Super Pinto. Tragedy struck on 4 May 1990 when the* Red Knight *crashed, killing Frank Sanders and a passenger.*

mission was eventually overtaken by the Cessna T–37 and Northrop T–38, but the T–33 remained active in USAF and ANG service, performing the role of hack, target tug, proficiency trainer and so on. It was with a great deal of sadness that the last USAF/ANG T-Bird was retired in 1988. Unfortunately, there was no single aircraft that could assume its role and the passing of the T-Bird has left a big blank.

Some of the retired ANG T-Birds had been operating with their units since new—an amazing record of reliability! Virtually all of the retired aircraft were reassigned to Third World nations south of the border. These aircraft were reconfigured as AT–33s, equipped with two Browning .50 caliber machine guns and underwing hard points. The government "sold" them to the Latin American nations for $12,000 apiece. "Several pilots tried to purchase their aircraft," commented one ANG pilot, "but the government refused to release the planes to fly under civilian registration."

Quite a few air forces still operate the T-Bird, especially Canada. It plans

to keep its seventy-odd T-Birds flying until the year 2010.

On the current jet warbird market, the T-33 is the most numerous type and functions in a variety of roles from flight test to pleasure flying. The first civil-registered T-33 appeared during the late 1950s and was built from surplus parts, since obtaining an entire airframe was nearly impossible for a civilian at that time. This first civil T-Bird was pretty lonely since civilian-owned jet warbirds were almost unheard of during the early 1960s.

NASA became a user of the T-Bird along with, oddly enough, the FAA which had a few aircraft in civil registration. Interestingly, the FAA fleet quickly disappeared as FAA pilots managed to damage or destroy their T-Birds in short order.

During the 1960s, Flight Test Research (FTR) was established at Long Beach Airport. Specializing in the flight test of products that required high-performance jet aircraft, FTR obtained several former RCAF T-Birds that were civilianized and turned into experimental test platforms. FTR was eventually reorganized into Flight Systems, the large test, modification and research company based at Mojave, California. Flight Systems acquired other former RCAF T-33s and put the planes to a wide variety of use, including one aircraft that mounted a retractable

*The T-33 was developed from the Lockheed P-80 fighter. Unfortunately, no flying examples of the P-80 exist. However, in the 1970s, an attempt was made to get one of the planes flyable. Dick Martin took the hulk of a Columbian Air Force F-80C and mated it with parts from a crashed FAA T-33B, N156. Unfortunately, this ambitious project, registered N10DM, did not progress much further after this photograph taken in July 1972 at Van Nuys Airport.*

water-dispensing boom that was used to dump water onto aircraft trailing in formation to test for ice-buildup effects.

T-Birds became more available to private owners in the 1970s. Warbird owner and pilot Leroy Penhall imported several Canadair-built T–33s (the Canadians called their planes Silver Stars) in the early years of the decade. These aircraft were run through Penhall's facility at Chino, California, and emerged as very attractive, practical jet warbirds that were snapped up by well-heeled private pilots. Usually painted in bright colors, the Penhall T-Birds were at the forefront of the new jet warbird movement.

More and more T-Birds began to show up on the civil register as aircraft were imported from foreign sources and rebuilt from surplus airframes already in the United States. The T-Bird is useful rapid personal transportation for two (although the engine will eat up over 800 gallons per hour at full throttle!). It also can perform in the role for which it was designed: as a trainer. Many jet warbird pilots have used the T-Bird as an effective training platform before moving on to higher-performance equipment.

T-Bird owners like Ray Mabrey of Coon Rapids, Michigan, enjoy campaigning their aircraft around the country and visiting airshows. Ray has his plane painted in a wild Thunderbird-style scheme that is certainly eye catching. "The T-Bird is a practical jet warbird," states Ray. "Since it has simple systems, can be easily worked on, and has a very large base of spare engine and airframe parts."

Another very colorful T-Bird is a Canadair-built example operated by Rick Brickert and Dennis and Frank Sanders. All three pilots are well known on the airshow scene, and they decided that a jet aerobatic act would be just the thing to inject some new excitement in flying performances. They obtained their T-Bird from another owner and then completely went through it to ensure the aircraft was in perfect operation condition.

Airshows are big business and it's a business that definitely shows a growth trend. Rick, Frank and Dennis wanted to create an innovative act so they installed Sanders Smokewinders in the T-Bird's wingtip tanks. Anyone who has attended an international airshow has probably seen an F–16 aerobatic act equipped with Smokewinders. The units produce prodigious quantities of smoke, making the flying act much more visible and exciting for the spectator.

"We do a real tight airshow in order to keep the jet in front of the crowd at all times, and that smoke is really an extra plus," said Rick. "Most airshows do not have the funds to contract with a military team for an airshow performance but our aircraft can offer many of the same thrills at a much more reasonable price and we all know that jets pull really big at airshows."

The trio had been impressed by photos they had seen of an RCAF Silver Star operated as an aerobatic ship during the late 1950s and 1960s. "We really liked the bright red paint and name *Red Knight*," said Rick. "So we decided to style our aircraft after the RCAF *Red Knight*."

In 1958, the RCAF gave approval to the solo aerobatic T-Bird that would carry the name *Red Knight*. The main reason for this presentation was to carry the RCAF presence to smaller communities where the RCAF's Golden Hawks aerobatic team could not perform with their Sabres. The *Red Knight* operated from 1958 through 1969 (by mid 1968, the T-Bird was replaced with a Tutor). A number of aircraft were utilized as the *Red Knight*—several were destroyed in accidents. One of the original *Red Knights*, 21574, is preserved

*NX333JM is an attractively finished Canadair-built Mk. 3 (RCAF serial number 21456) that was photographed in June 1984 with test pilot Neil Anderson in the front cockpit and owner Jimmie McMillan in the rear seat.*

*Here's another view of RCAF serial number 21456 taken in September 1983 when it was owned by Matt Jackson (as N333MJ) and finished in USAF markings for the film* The Right Stuff. *Dave Zeuschel flies wing in his newly restored F–86F N86Z.*

*Over the years, civilian T-Birds have appeared in a wide variety of creative color schemes. One of the most interesting is N155X which was photographed at Chino, California, in October 1982. Owned at the time by Aeronautical Test Vehicles, N155X first appeared on the US civil register during 1965. A former RCAF Mk. 3 (serial number 21157), this aircraft is now registered N133AT and flies in an overall black color scheme.*

and displayed at the National Aeronautical Collection in Ottawa.

Starting their airshow routine in 1989, the *Red Knight* has been extremely successful and has performed around the nation.

As we enter the 1990s, T-Birds in very good condition can be purchased for between $100,000 and $150,000—a bargain when compared to a P–51 Mustang. As several foreign air forces prepare to phase out their T-Bird fleets, it appears likely that more T-Birds will appear on the civil register as the warbird movement expands with the addition of this classic and practical jet.

## Chapter 5

# Grumman Panther

The Grumman Panther started life in a rather curious manner. The US Navy, toward the end of World War II, realized the jet age was fast approaching. Not having the luxury of unlimited runway lengths and having to key most considerations toward carrier operations, the Navy and Grumman attempted to design a night fighter with the latest technology available. Unfortunately, about all that was available was the rather anemic Westinghouse J30 of 1,500 lbs. static thrust. Final design work began in early 1946 and the envisioned aircraft was to have been powered by four of these little screamers—probably giving marginal performance while creating a maintenance nightmare. This original Panther design was never built.

Fortunately, Grumman imported a Rolls-Royce Nene that could pump out a respectable 5,000 lbs. of thrust. A redesign took place and the resulting aircraft, the XF9F-2, flew for the first time on 24 November 1947.

In order to develop a second engine source (a common US practice after the British had canceled America's license agreement with Packard to build the Rolls-Royce Merlin when World War II concluded), an Allison J33-A-8 of 4,600 lbs. thrust was installed in the XF9F-3 which was basically identical to the -2. The -3 flew for the first time on 16 August 1948.

The Navy issued a contract for forty-seven F9F-2s and fifty-four F9F-3s and the service was well on its way into the jet age. Testing in the field showed the Navy preferred the Nene-powered -2, and all -3s were eventually converted to that engine. Grumman had

built 520 more F9F-2s by mid 1951 and the type was active with many front line squadrons.

Basically a "first and a half" generation jet aircraft, the Panther (as the type had been named in order to stick with Grumman's line of famous naval "cats") did not really have world class jet fighter performance. The plane, like all Grummans, was rugged and honest—packing a heavy punch with four 20 mm cannon buried under the nose and the capability of carrying six five-inch rockets or two 500 lb. bombs under the wings. Two wingtip fuel tanks were permanently mounted to cater to the jet's heavy thirst (the engine was being built under license by Pratt & Whitney as the J42-P-6, all worries about canceled license agreements having been worked out).

When Communist forces moved against South Korea, the Panther almost immediately went into action against the hordes of troops overrunning Allied forces. Launched from carriers off shore, the Panther proved to be a solid ground-attack mount and its heavy armament took unbelievable tolls of the enemy. The Panthers were quite often fuel limited in their attacks

*Although underpowered, the Grumman F9F-2 Panther had clean and simple lines that made for a very attractive airplane. Originally designed as a four-jet night fighter, the concept was changed to a single-engine day fighter when more powerful engines became available. The F9F-2 owned and flown by Arthur Wolk is the finest example of its type.*

*F9F-2 BuNo 123072 was originally restored from two Panther hulks by William Pryor and Jack Levine, who is seen flying the aircraft. NX72WP is fitted with underwing five-inch rockets and can also carry two 500 lb. dummy bombs. The Panther originally had four 20 mm cannon and Pryor and Levine installed non-firing replicas in their restoration.*

but mission after mission was flown against the enemy. (An excellent portrayal of Panther pilots in combat is available in the Paramount film *Bridges of Toko-Ri.*)

As Allied air forces slowly began to exert their influence and got the North Koreans on the run, the Russians and Red Chinese unleashed a

nasty little surprise: The MiG-15 air superiority fighter.

The British, undertaking a bit of shameless capitalism, had sold some Nenes to the Soviets who quickly copied the powerplant for inclusion in their new fighter which was being built in secret. The MiG-15 proved to be a dangerous enemy, roaring into boxed formations of B-29s and decimating the once almost invulnerable bomber (the Superforts quickly switched to night operations).

Even USAF fighters—Lockheed F-80 Shooting Stars and North American F-51 Mustangs—and Navy fighters and fighter-bombers—Grumman F9F Panthers, Douglas AD Skyraiders and Vought F4U Corsairs—were at the mercy of the MiG. However, an F9F-2

scored the Navy's first jet-versus-jet victory on 9 November 1950. Lt. Cmdr. W. T. Amen of VF-111 blasted a MiG-15 with the plane's 20 mm cannon. But it was not until the introduction of the North American F-86F Sabre that Americans once again took complete control of the air. Even then the MiG was a real threat if in the hands of a good pilot.

Throughout the extensive and vicious air actions over Korea, Panthers flew over 78,000 missions against the enemy. After the F9F-2, several other variants of the Panther with increasingly powerful engines were built. The design culminated in the F9F-6 Cougar, a swept-wing, upgraded redesign of the Panther. After Korea, Panthers were rapidly replaced in front line

units with newer aircraft but Panthers did soldier on with the Naval Air Reserve—giving some pilots their first taste of jet combat aircraft.

As with many other American aircraft of the period, the Panthers, once their active service days were over, were quickly turned into pots and pans. Stripped of useful equipment, the bare airframes were sold off in large lots to scrappers who hacked the planes apart and stuffed them into smelters in order to reclaim aluminum and other valuable metals. A few Panthers were transferred to foreign air forces like Argentina, some were given to civilian parks to become playtoys for children—who quickly wrought a form of destruction on the planes that even the Communists couldn't.

During the 1970s, the collecting, restoring and flying of vintage World War II aircraft increased in popularity. Many businesses sprung up that specialized in the rebuilding and maintenance of these historic machines. Also, an expanding interest in aviation at this time meant that more airshows were created to meet public demand. Airshow promoters quickly found out one of the most popular attractions was the display and flying of these wonderful vintage machines—aircraft that were classified under the generic name of warbirds.

As the very limited supplies of surviving propeller-driven fighters and bombers began to dry up, some restorers began looking at other former military aircraft—including vintage jets.

*The restorers managed to find photographs of their aircraft in service with VF–112 during the Korean War and the markings were painstakingly reproduced on the restoration. The Panther is shown in formation with a Fouga Magister two-seat trainer/attack aircraft.*

Restorers were disappointed by the fact that these vintage warriors seemed to simply not exist or that the few available airframes were in such poor condition that it would cost a fortune to get the planes back into airworthy condition.

Two warbird enthusiasts, Jack Levine and William Pryor, were not going to be put off by the difficulty of

47

recreating a vintage combat jet. They formed a partnership and obtained two F9F–2 Panther hulks. One aircraft came from a gas station in Oklahoma where it had been on display for over two decades; the other example came from the Philadelphia Navy Yard where it had presided over the scrap heap for years. Both airframes were transported to Pryor's Ly-Con Aviation hangar at Pontiac, Michigan, where the airframes were stripped and inspected.

Finding Panther parts was a problem and the pair burned up the phone lines as they called around the country, trying to find vital bits and pieces. Fortunately, a Pratt & Whitney J42–P–6 engine was obtained from a museum and a thorough check showed the engine was usable with some rebuilding.

Both men wanted to make the Panther as original as possible, but a few concessions were in order so the plane could be taken to airshows across the country; a modern avionics suite was installed including LORAN-C, King Gold Crown avionics, and other systems necessary for safe cross-country travel. Replicas were constructed of the Panther's four 20 mm cannon (using many original parts but making sure the weapons could never fire, to meet federal regulations) while static examples of the underwing five-inch rockets and 500 lb. high-explosive bombs were obtained.

The restoration took an intense four years and Levine made the first post-restoration flight in 1983. The usual first-flight problems were encountered, and the Panther went back into the hangar for some fine-tuning and painting in the colors of the US Navy's VF–112 fighter squadron that saw combat in Korea. This paint scheme is beautiful, authentic *and* appropriate because the airframe that was restored (bureau number 123072) saw service with VF–112 in Korea. The experimental civil-registration NX72WP was obtained from the Federal Aviation Administration (FAA).

In 1984, Levine took the Panther to the aviation gathering at Oshkosh, Wisconsin, and the magnificently restored jet was awarded the Warbird Grand Champion trophy by the Experimental Aircraft Association. Levine took the plane to many other airshows, where it was a very popular display. Levine once commented that, "It's easier to ship the rockets and two 500 lb. bombs to the more distant airshows I'm attending. With all that ordnance attached, the Panther really slows down and the fuel consumption skyrockets."

Levine was also an enthusiastic owner of a North American P–51D Mustang which he had flown for many years. During an outing in this aircraft, he failed to recover from a low-altitude aerobatic maneuver and slammed into the ground—killing himself and a passenger. Shortly afterward, the Panther was put up for sale.

The purchaser was Arthur Wolk of Philadelphia. Wolk, an attorney specializing in aviation matters, had flown general aviation aircraft but was new to the warbird field. He had always admired such aircraft and felt that the historic Panther would be an ideal aircraft for fun flying and airshow work.

Wolk enjoys taking the F9F–2 to various air meets around the country but finds that the plane is distinctly underpowered (5,000 lbs. of thrust for a 16,000 lb. fully-loaded Panther) and he has to carefully manage his fuel supply, airfield lengths and so on. Takeoff distances can vary between 4,000 and 6,000 feet, depending on load, altitude and temperature. Initial acceleration with ninety-eight percent engine thrust is sluggish, but once takeoff is achieved and the aircraft cleaned up, performance improves with a 4,500 foot per minute (fpm) rate of climb at 230 knots.

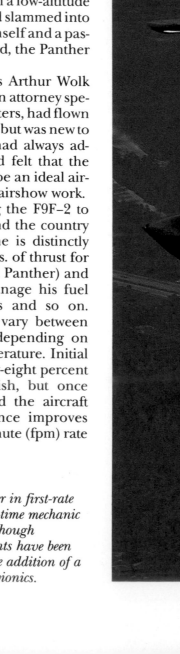

*Wolk maintains the Panther in first-rate condition courtesy of a full-time mechanic assigned to the aircraft. Although extremely stock, improvements have been made in the cockpit with the addition of a complete suite of modern avionics.*

With wingtip tanks, the military –2s carried 923 gallons of usable JP–4 fuel but, during restoration, a new aluminum fuel tank was built from scratch and this reduced the fuel load by some forty-three gallons. If flying under 10,000 feet, fuel burns can be as much as 600 gallons per hour—improving to about 375 gph at 25,000 feet. However, there is a tradeoff since, as Levine once commented, "Performance above 20,000 ft. is pretty marginal when the underwing stores are installed, and to get that high takes some time since the rate of climb drops to about 700 fpm after passing through 12,000 ft."

Arthur Wolk does not plan flight legs longer than 600 miles and tries to plan his flights at high altitude in order to conserve fuel. Operating costs (including fuel, maintenance and so on) are about $2,000 per flight hour.

Mechanic Frank Baldo is employed by Wolk to handle all the maintenance on the Panther, and he keeps the plane in perfect condition. Wolk has also built up a store of Panther airframe and engine parts. One interesting point is that the ejection seat is non-operational, since the early "hot" seats used in the aircraft often inflicted spinal damage on the ejecting pilot.

Harry Doan also has a flyable F9F–2 located in New Smyrna Beach, Florida, but this Panther is nowhere near the mint condition of Wolk's plane. It is, however, occasionally flown and may eventually be restored to show condition. A two-seat Grumman F9F–8T Cougar is being restored to flying condition in Florida by Don Whittington and is one of two such aircraft delivered to Argentina in the 1960s.

*Currently, only one other Panther remains in flying condition. This aircraft, registered N9525A, is owned by Harry Doan in New Smyrna Beach, Florida. Although it is nowhere as pristine as Wolk's aircraft, the Panther is still flying.*

# Chapter 6

# Mikoyan-Gurevich MiGs

One of the most curious global trends of the late 1980s was the gradual opening of Communist countries to Western visitors and trade. While it is still much too early for historians to comment on the far-ranging effects of this change, one fact that we can report and speculate upon is the import of large quantities of former Soviet combat aircraft designs into this country for use as jet warbirds.

The first interest in selling surplus warplanes to the West came from the People's Republic of China. During the mid 1980s, China began to warm to Western ways, allowing various business concerns to set up offices, factories and hotels in mainland China. Tourism increased and it became popular to visit China and view the many historic sites in that ancient country. American warbird buffs quickly discovered that there were interesting vintage military aircraft in China—lots of them.

The Chinese tend to be fairly formal about their dealings, but it did not take long for the Americans to find middlemen for their MiG purchases. The Chinese were a bit puzzled as to why the Americans wanted what they considered obsolete aircraft. But they were not going to quarrel with the infusion of greenbacks—especially in a nation that was starving for foreign currency.

The first major jet warbird deal involved a group of MiG–15s—Korean War era fighters that had caused a great deal of trouble for Allied forces. These aircraft were not Russian-built. The MiGs had been built at the Shenyang factory starting in 1954 and had last been assigned to a training unit with the Chinese Navy before being withdrawn from service. The MiGs were in exceptionally fine condition, considering their age, and a deal was struck that would see the planes transported to Chino, California.

America and its allies had viewed the Soviets as a threatening, but rather primitive, force after the conclusion of World War II. When the United States and its United Nations allies entered the Korean War in 1950, it became obvious that the American military had been allowed to run down in those short five years. American F–51s, F–80s and F–84s suddenly encountered a new fighter being flown by the enemy—a fighter that had completely slipped past the so-called military intelligence network. Simply put, the new aircraft was good, very good, and was causing a tremendous amount of damage to the United Nation's air forces.

In 1946, Stalin demanded a new fighter that would give the Soviets an effective jet warplane. The specifications required for this new plane included a top speed of over 620 mph, a ceiling of over 45,000 ft., pressurized cockpit, ejection seat, the ability to carry heavy armament, participate in ground attack missions and operate from unimproved airfields. Clearly, Stalin was expecting a lot from his designers—men who knew that an unpleasant fate awaited them if they failed.

Utilizing a great deal of captured German data on advanced swept-wing aerodynamics, the design teams of Artem I. Mikoyan and Mikhail I. Gurevich came up with a stubby-looking little fighter that had a swept-back wing and tail, was simple in construction but was limited by the lack of a suitable powerplant. The use of former Luftwaffe Jumo turbojets just did not give enough reliable power. The Soviets set up a trade mission to Britain and made a deal to procure Rolls-Royce engines (twenty-five Nenes and thirty Derwents). Britain has, unfortunately, been a nation with a policy of selling to anyone with money and, considering the number of Soviet moles that had infiltrated the British government during this time period, it is not surprising this deal went through—a transaction that would come back to haunt them.

Once the Soviets had their hands on the Nenes, they immediately went to work to make an exact copy for the new fighter. The first prototype equipped with a British-built Nene flew on 30 December 1947. Of simple construction, the prototype was fairly docile but exhibited a few negative characteristics like falling into a spin when too much G was applied in a turn. The spin was recoverable but a great deal of altitude was lost in the recovery process and the Allies would later prey upon this weakness.

The new type was designated MiG–15 and was the fighter Stalin wanted. Rushed into production, the MiG–15 would be produced in many different variants for the Soviets and their many allies. Although exact figures are unavailable, it appears over 5,000 MiG–15s were built. By the end of

*Want a MiG–17 restoration project? This former Chinese example is seen awaiting a buyer at Chino Airport.*

Previous page
*In the air, the MiG-15 is quite an attractive aircraft with an arrow-like shape. On the ground, however, the barrel fuselage and short landing gear give the fighter a tubby appearance.*

*On its first test flight after restoration by Unlimited Aircraft Ltd., test pilot Norman Suits positions former Chinese Navy MiG-15bis N90601 for the camera plane. This aircraft was purchased by Paul Entrekin and later registered N15PE (Chinese serial number 122073). The large registration was required by the FAA for all flight test work.*

1949, the MiG-15bis (*bis* standing for modified or second series) was pressed into production. This variant had better overall performance and went on to be produced in Hungary, Poland, Czechoslovakia and China.

When the Americans encountered the MiG-15 in November 1950, tactics had to be quickly changed. For example, the once mighty B-29 Superfortress was now easy prey for the enemy jets and the USAF had to change its bombing raids to operate under the protective cover of darkness. The North American F-86E and F Sabre were rushed into production and sent to Japan and Korea as soon as available. These aircraft began to turn the tables on the MiG. Actually, it was probably due more to the Americans' superior combat training since both aircraft, being flown by skilled pilots, were fairly matched with the MiG having the advantage in climb, dive speed, roll rate, ceiling and heavier armament (one 37 mm N-37 cannon with forty rounds and two 23 mm NS-23 cannon with eighty rounds each).

By the end of the war, the USAF claimed a total of 792 MiGs destroyed

for the loss of seventy-eight Sabres. This was a bit unrealistic and more recent studies have narrowed the gap slightly, but there is no doubt that the aggressive Sabre pilots slaughtered the MiGs.

After the questionable peace agreement that brought an end to the Korean War, MiGs operated in huge numbers with all of the Soviet allies. Their sheer numbers, alone, posed a problem for NATO planners.

Many of the countries operating the MiG–15s have a habit of not throwing things away or scrapping older bits of military hardware—unlike the more affluent Western nations. China held vast reserves of older military equipment, and American warbird collectors were thrilled by the discovery of previously unknown airframes.

The initial batch of Chinese MiGs arrived at Chino Airport in 1986 to Unlimited Aircraft Ltd., a well-known warbird rebuilder. Examination of the MiGs proved the aircraft to be in exceptional condition—the planes even arrived with armament intact (soon to be removed by ATF officials and offered to suitable museums) and were encased in individually hand-sewn canvas covers to protect the airframes during their long sea voyage.

*The Chinese MiGs were delivered to the States with full armament. The three cannon on Paul Entrekin's MiG were removed by the ATF and donated to the National Air and Space Museum. This view of the MiG was one often seen by F-86 Sabre pilots during the Korean War. The Sabres built up a phenomenal kill ratio over the enemy aircraft during aerial combat.*

As rebuilding of the craft started, they were put up for sale and advertised in various aeronautical journals—bringing a steady stream of visitors to

Unlimited's vintage World War II hangar. Actually, the main problem getting the planes registered and flying was with the manuals and not the airframes. The manuals had to be very carefully translated for FAA regulations and considerable money was spent with the University of California getting a correct and usable translation.

One of the MiGs was purchased by Paul Entrekin, a former Marine pilot and now a pilot with Delta Airlines. Entrekin didn't want his MiG to be a personal toy, but rather wanted to put the vintage fighter to work doing airshows. Once the plane was licensed, he did exactly that and his shows have been very popular. The MiG is finished in the markings of a Soviet "volunteer" unit that flew with the North Koreans during the war, and Entrekin plays the part by dressing in a Russian outfit. When obtained, this MiG had only about 1,800 flying hours logged.

Before flying the MiG, Entrekin got some dual instruction in a civilian T–33A. The MiG has had some of the instruments replaced with American units and a set of King radios added. Entrekin found the MiG fairly easy to fly, the most difficult part being the use of the rather primitive pneumatic differential braking system which he may replace with a hydraulic unit.

Other MiG–15s are currently flying, including the beautifully maintained example operated by the Combat Jets Flying Museum. Also a Chinese Navy example rebuilt by Unlimited, this aircraft is fitted with a smoke system and is often flown in "combat" at airshows with one of the two Sabres owned by the museum.

Importation of MiGs has not been without problems. China was on a favored trade status with the Ameri-

*This MiG–17F, N1VC, owned by jet warbird collector Morgan Merrill, is seen at Chino Airport following a complete restoration. The MiG–17 is a growth variant of the –15 and was an excellent interceptor in its day.*

59

cans until the 1989 student protest incident. However, nations like Hungary and Poland were not on such a status and old, vague laws disallowed the importation of anything like former combat jet aircraft.

This situation came to a head in mid 1989 after the respected Planes of Fame Air Museum imported a MiG–15, MiG–17 and an Antonov An–2 (a large, ponderous biplane) for display in their museum. Since these aircraft came from countries on the "forbidden" list, a huge battle arose. The planes passed all US Customs checks, but the US Bureau of Alcohol, Tobacco and Firearms (ATF) objected when they discovered the planes were in the museum. ATF forced Customs to admit they had made a "mistake" by allowing the planes into the country, even though all the paperwork had been correctly filled out. ATF then demanded the planes be given to the US government at no cost or immediately scrapped on site!

Needless to say, this angered the museum and a petition was drawn up to save the aircraft—well over 7,000 signatures from airplane lovers were obtained. ATF stuck to its position (ignoring the fact that relations with these nations were rapidly changing and that their manufactured incident was becoming embarrassing on an international scale). The situation looked pretty dark until congressmen Jerry Lewis and Robert K. Dornan stepped in to help pass a bill that saved the day

*Some of the many MiGs at Classics In Aviation, Stead Airport, Reno, Nevada. The company has supplied a variety of MiGs to civilian as well as military owners.*

Next page
*Is a freshly restored MiG–15 more your line? Pristine N90859 could be yours. MiG prices range from $100,000 to $250,000 depending on condition, number of flying hours and so forth.*

THE HUFF

4115

for the museum. However, the bill was not a blanket opening to the import of aircraft from these countries but a very specific legislation that applied only to these aircraft.

Other MiGs have been entering the country quite regularly. At Stead Airport in Reno, Nevada, Classics In Aviation have imported a large batch of Polish MiGs. This company has apparently avoided problems with ATF by supplying a number of their airframes to the US military.

Classics In Aviation has supplied MiG–15s, –17s, –21s and other non-jet Soviet aircraft to the Defense Department to form part of a Capability Improvement Program put forth by John Krings, director of the Pentagon's Operational Test and Evaluation Program. Apparently reasoning that the use of such equipment will provide realistic training for US forces, the Defense Test and Support Evaluation Agency (DTESA) would like to acquire enough Soviet aircraft, radars, support equipment and missiles to equip a two-regiment Soviet force that can be utilized by all US services for training.

The USAF has long operated a secret MiG unit based in Nevada for training purposes and these aircraft were acquired through clandestine methods (mainly coming through Indonesia and Middle East sources) and remain classified even though photographs of MiG–21s in USAF markings have appeared in the popular press. With the thawing of relations between the United States and the Soviet Union along with cutbacks in military spending, it is doubtful whether this program will progress to DTESA's ambitious conclusion. Also, it is doubtful that such ancient equipment could really provide much in the way of realistic training, unless DTESA has plans to

*Paul "Geraldo" Entrekin flies Combat Jets' MiG–15bis N15MG while Chuck Scott flies wing in the Sabre. N15MG is equipped for a smoke system for airshow work.*

Previous page
*Powered by a Klimov VK–1 turbojet of 6,000 lbs. thrust, the MiG–15bis can achieve Mach 0.94 (670 mph) and has a cruise range of 1,200 miles with drop tanks. Span is 33 ft. 1 in., length is 36 ft. 5 in., and the MiG stands 11 ft. 2 in. tall.*

take on Third World nations that still operate such aircraft.

Other aircraft like MiG–17s, –19s and –21s are coming onto the civil register. Dean Martin has imported several MiG–17s, an improved variant of the –15, from China via the China Ocean Helicopter Corporation. "I had a hell of time getting the Feds to register the MiG–17s," said Martin. "But they are now licensed and flying. Nobody in the FAA wanted to put their name on the airworthiness certificate since there weren't any flying in the country. They're legal and flying now. Perform like rocket ships, you just stand it on the tail and climb. They're great interceptors. Wanna buy one?"

High-performance MiG–21s have also made their appearance. Classics In Aviation in Reno has several. Combat Jets Flying Museum has obtained a Chinese MiG–21 and has rebuilt the plane to their usual exacting standards. There is a good chance this aircraft, which saw so much combat in Vietnam, will be flying by the end of 1990. With all the opening trade doors between America and former Communist countries, there is little doubt that we will be seeing more and more red stars over the States.

*With a moon on the nose, Entrekin displays the MiG–15's 35 degree wing sweep and the armament installation of the three cannon.*

# Chapter 7

# North American Sabre

Simply put, the North American F–86 Sabre is one of the United States' most successful jet fighters.

With the defeat of Germany in 1945, there was a mad scramble to recover German engineering and technical data on a wide variety of subjects—everything from medical experiments to aeronautics. There was little disagreement among the Allies that the majority of these data were very worthwhile and no effort was spared in obtaining the material. American forces realized it was essential the majority of the documentation escape Soviet attention. By daring individual actions the United States managed to obtain a significant portion of German aeronautical and rocket data, along with capturing key scientists that had been involved with important projects.

Propeller-driven fighters had run into an invisible barrier in the sky—one that their designs could not penetrate. The German jet and rocket force had penetrated this barrier and were offering huge leaps in performance over the Allied fighters. Even the new

*During 1980, Dave Zeuschel and John Sandberg recovered one of the last F–86F Sabres from the Peruvian Air Force. The plane was transported back to Chino where it was restored to airworthy condition as N86F (USAF serial number 52–5139). In November 1981, N86F was equipped with Sanders Smokewinders on the underwing pylons for testing. The Smokewinders can be seen belching out vast quantities of colored smoke. The Sabre, at this time, was in the markings of Aviation Systems International.*

generation of Allied aircraft like the Meteor, Vampire and Shooting Star did not have the design sophistication of some of the German types.

The Germans had accrued data on the effects of compressibility as an aircraft approached the sound barrier. They found they could move the compressibility barrier forward by utilizing swept wings and other aeronautical modifications. True, the sound barrier was still out of their reach but German aircraft were now operating much closer to that magic figure than their Allied counterparts. In combat aviation, speed almost always equals victory.

Captured data were rapidly brought back to the United States, translated and dispersed to appropriate aviation concerns. North American Aviation had enjoyed an amazingly successful run of combat aircraft during World War II, including the AT–6 Texan, B–25 Mitchell and P–51 Mustang. With creative management by Dutch Kindleberger and engineering skill from Edgar Schmued and others, the company quickly grasped the opportunity of producing an advanced jet warplane.

The project would be designated NA–140 and, from the start, would utilize captured data to the fullest. The design had all its flying surfaces swept, and the overall airframe was beautifully clean. Ordered as the XP–86 on

Next page
*Wearing the colorful markings carried by Lt. Jim Thompson's Korean War Sabre, N8687D is flown here by Chuck Scott.*

18 May 1945, construction rapidly progressed and the prototype made its first flight from Muroc Dry Lake on 1 October 1947.

Powered by a J35–C–3 turbojet built by Chevrolet and producing 3,750 lbs. of thrust, the new aircraft was a winner from the start. So impressed was the Air Force that they placed orders for thirty-three P–86As on 20 December 1946. As usual, powerplant design was running behind airframe construction. After the first P–86A flew on 20 May 1948, 333 more aircraft were ordered but these planes had to make due with a variety of engine types (J47–GE–1, GE–3, GE–7) until the full production GE–13 was ready for installation. The GE–13 pumped out 5,200 lbs. of thrust and enabled the fighter to really come into its own.

The Sabre, as the type was appropriately named, had a thirty-five-degree sweep to its wings and horizontal stabilizer. Armament consisted of six .50 caliber Brownings placed in the nose, with three on each side of the intake. The choice of the machine gun for armament is curious since, by this time, the British and Europeans had settled on heavy cannon armament for their jet fighters.

The USAF wanted to show what their hot new fighter could do. The third F–86A–1 was groomed for a series of speed runs and on 1 September 1948 set a new record of 670.98 mph (jet records were coming fast and furious in those heady days).

Beside the armament of Brownings (each gun had 267 rounds), the F–86A could also handle two 120 gallon drop tanks, two 1,000 lb. bombs or sixteen rockets on underwing mounts.

Production of the A model Sabre totaled 554 aircraft, concluding in De-

*Combat Jets Flying Museum based at Houston-Hobby Airport in Texas maintains two Canadair Sabres in flying condition. One aircraft, N8687D, is finished in very accurate Korean War markings while the other, N86JR, is finished in civil colors.*

*Certainly one of the most distinctive paint schemes applied to a Sabre was the metallic gold and red design carried by the RCAF's Golden Hawks aerobatic team. Flight Test Research, based at Long Beach, California, obtained two of the Golden Hawks' distinctive aircraft during 1965 for flight test projects. N186F (RCAF 23454, CF-AMH) and N186X (RCAF 23434), both Mk. 6 Sabres, are seen at Long Beach on 12 December 1967. The two aircraft passed to Flight Systems at Mojave and may have been destroyed as drones.*

cember 1950, and aircraft were rapidly dispersed to operational units—many of which had been flying the Lockheed F–80. The 1st Fighter Group at March AFB, California, received their A mod-

els in February 1949, closely followed by the 4th and 81st Fighter Groups.

With the start of the Korean War and the appearance of the hitherto unknown MiG–15, Sabres were rushed to Korea to counter the new threat. Even though the MiGs were not flown by overly skilled pilots, they managed to knock down forty-two F–51 Mustangs, F–80 Shooting Stars and F–84 Thunderjets for a loss of fifteen of their own in a short time. Twenty-three B–26 Invaders and B–29 Superfortresses were also destroyed (their gunners claimed sixteen MiGs), quickly proving the superiority of the swept-wing fighter in aerial combat.

Once the A model reached combat, it became apparent the plane suffered defects in a number of areas and North American rushed a new variant

of the Sabre into production that would be more suitable for combat. The F–86E had a power-operated movable tail surface but was otherwise similar to late production A models that were equipped with J47–GE–13 engines. It was the F–86F that really brought the Sabre into the winner's circle. Equipped with a J47–GE–27 of 5,910 lbs. thrust, the F could carry four underwing drop tanks or two tanks and two 1,000 lb. bombs. The wing was modified to replace the E's slats with an extended leading edge which improved maneuverability and speed. The F–86F was a welcome addition and MiGs began to fall in large numbers from withering blasts of lead from the Sabre's nose.

Some As and Fs were modified as recon platforms equipped with cam-

76

eras and given RF designations. The basic design also formed the basis for the rather unattractive F–86D "Sabredog" night fighter (which had originally been designated F–95 and should have remained that way since the plane differed in so many aspects from the F–86). Two dual-control TF–86Fs were also built but it was apparently decided to leave the training mission to the T–33, which was a shame since TF–86 was quite attractive and versatile.

The F–86H was the first variant designed as a fighter bomber. The H was equipped with four 20 mm cannon with 150 rounds each. The H could carry a large variety of underwing weapons including nuclear bombs.

The Sabre was also built under license by several countries, the first being Canada. Built by Canadair in Montreal, the first example was a US F–86A assembled from parts as the Sabre Mk. 1. This was followed by 350 Mk. 2s, 438 Mk. 4s, one Mk. 3, 370 Mk. 5s and 655 Mk. 6s. The Mk. 5 featured the Orenda 10 turbojet with 6,355 lbs. thrust while the Mk. 6 had the 7,275 lb. thrust Orenda 14. Besides serving with the RCAF, Canadair Sabres were supplied to many countries inside and outside of NATO.

In Australia, Commonwealth Aircraft built 111 CA–27 Sabres that had been extensively modified to incorporate the Rolls-Royce Avon of 7,500 lbs. thrust and two heavy-hitting Aden 30 mm cannon. The CA–27 was a real tiger and USAF Phantom pilots who did air combat maneuvering with the

*During the early 1970s, Ben Hall of Seattle, Washington, began the difficult task of creating a flyable F–86A Sabre from several hulks. The early Sabre differs from later variants in a number of ways and N68388 is the only flying example of its type. The aircraft is seen at the 1980 Reno Air Races where it wore the distinctive markings of its television sponsor. Hall later modified the aircraft to have a second seat (under the same canopy). The F–86A was sold to a British owner in 1990.*

RAAF Sabre reported that it was a very tough opponent.

In Japan, Mitsubishi received 300 sets of components to construct F–86Fs along with 206 flyable F models.

*In 1983, Dave Zeuschel finished a meticulous restoration of an F–86F Sabre he had discovered in a California apple orchard barn. Registered N86Z, the bare metal Sabre is seen on a test flight in July 1983 accompanied by freshly restored P–51D Mustang N6175C with Skip Holm piloting.*

After use by these nations, Sabres went on to serve with many Third World nations and saw considerable action, such as the September 1965 war between India (flying British Gnats) and Pakistan (flying Sabres).

As well as supplying large numbers of Sabres to overseas customers, the USAF scrapped many aircraft at Davis-Monthan after they finished service (Sabres operated faithfully with many Air National Guard units). Other Sabres were released to become monuments or gate guardians, but the government was completely against letting civilians get their hands on what was considered an advanced fighter.

In 1967, Flight Test Research (FTR), based at Long Beach, California, purchased two former RCAF Golden Hawks Sabres and had the planes licensed in the experimental research and development category. FTR eventually changed its name to Flight Systems and homebase to Mojave Airport, and the company began importing large numbers of Canadian Sabres.

These planes, alas, were not destined for civilian ownership. FTR restored the Sabres to airworthy and civil-registered them with the FAA, but the planes were actually being modified into drones for the US Army—to be destroyed during weapons testing. Unfortunately, the demand for Sabres was so intense that Flight Systems purchased several nicely restored civilian examples and used them for drones (imagine that happening to another warbird like a P–51 Mustang!). The appetite for drones was so overwhelming that aircraft were acquired from as far away as Germany and South Africa.

During this time, the mid 1970s and early 1980s, interest in jet warbirds was increasing. Leroy Penhall imported several former RCAF Silver Stars and two Sabres to his Chino facility and had the aircraft beautifully refinished as exotic sport planes. Penhall's untimely death in the crash of a general aviation twin ended his company's business of rebuilding Sabres for the civilian market.

Soon, others began to join in the fun. In Seattle, Ben Hall built a magnificent F–86A Sabre from several hulks and began flying the classic jet regularly.

Several major aircraft companies saw the value of the Sabre as a chase plane. For example, Boeing purchased a Canadian Sabre and has used the craft for years to chase its airliners and military aircraft.

Flight Systems also used nondrone Sabres for a variety of test missions, along with a rare AF–1E Fury (the "carrier-qualified" Navy version of the F–86). A visitor to Mojave during this period would have been absolutely overwhelmed by the number of vintage Sabres on the flight line.

Well-known warbird owner and Merlin engine rebuilder Dave Zeuschel traveled with John Sandberg (developer of the ultra-slick *Tsunami* unlimited air racer) to Peru in the late 1970s where they purchased a former Peru-

*After test flying of N86Z concluded, Zeuschel decided to paint the Sabre in the colorful 4th Fighter Group markings of MiG ace Major J. J. Jabara. Seen during a May 1986 flight, the Sabre displays the distinctive yellow identification bands worn by the Group's Sabres.*

vian Air Force F–86F. The plane was transported back to Chino and rebuilt with the license N86F. Zeuschel decided he wanted his own Sabre and a search for a suitable airframe came to fruition when he found a former California ANG F model in the most unlikely of locations: inside a dusty barn in a California apple orchard!

*With start cart plugged in, N86Z prepares for another flight.*

Zeuschel transported the Sabre back to his engine shop in Sylmar, California, and spent several years rebuilding the plane back to absolutely pristine condition. He updated a number of the systems, added a new radio package and fitted the airframe with as many new parts as possible. The new parts were discovered in a nearby warehouse where they were going to be scrapped the next day! For the price of scrap, Zeuschel acquired a huge cache of Sabre goodies.

Skip "I'll fly anything" Holm did the test flying honors and pronounced the Sabre operational. Licensed N86Z, Zeuschel made his first flights in the jet

shortly afterward. Although he had over 1,000 hours Mustang time, he took instruction in a T–33A to get acquainted with jet operating procedures. Once the test flying had been worked off, the bare metal Sabre was painted in the colorful 4th Fighter Group markings of MiG ace Major J. J. Jabara. The Sabre became an immediate hit at airshows in the western United States and, since it was a highly visible aircraft, became an important symbol for the newly developing jet warbird movement.

While on the way to a warbird show at Shafter, California, N86Z suffered a complete compressor failure. Zeuschel managed to get the aircraft (which was becoming more and more uncontrollable due to the connected failure of the hydraulic system) on the Shafter runway with gear up but the

plane's speed was very high and a wing tank ripped off on the runway, causing the Sabre to cartwheel and explode. The loss of Dave Zeuschel was a major blow to the warbird community and one that is still felt today.

Several other Sabre restorations are going on in the United States. Some F models have been imported from Argentina and are being restored to flying condition, while Frank Sanders and Kermit Weeks have obtained Australian-built Sabres for rebuild to flying condition. And, of course, Combat Jets maintains two beautiful Canadair Sabres.

Unfortunately, the largest batch of Sabres in existence is rapidly being destroyed in yet another drone program. In order to test modern air-to-air missiles, a realistic target is needed to provide accurate performance parameters and information on how the missile system functions under specific conditions. In the late 1970s, the folks at the China Lake Naval Weapons Center (NWC) decided the Sabre would make an excellent aircraft for converting into a remote-controlled drone. A search revealed that a number of Sabres was available in foreign countries and these aircraft had initially been purchased with United States funded military credits. This meant that the operating country had to do one of three things: scrap the aircraft upon phasing them out of active service, buy the aircraft outright from Uncle Sam, or return the aircraft to United States control. Because of this agreement, the Navy was able to obtain about 200 F–86Fs from the air forces of Japan and Nationalist China.

One of the storage lots at China Lake was rapidly filled with carefully preserved Sabres as they arrived from the foreign operators. "The Sabres coming in from Japan were really nice machines," commented NWC's Dick Wright, who not only test flies the Sabres in the manned configuration but has also accumulated hundreds of hours operating the Fs as drones from his ground control station. "Some of the Japanese machines had as little as 1,500 hours total flying time along with very little corrosion. We picked the best aircraft for the first conversion to a drone and have followed that policy since."

The equipment for converting the Sabre to a drone was designed and developed by the Naval Weapons Center and then put out to contract. "Several companies did drone conversions for us," stated Wright. "However, about

*Sabres head-on. Paul Metz and Dick Wright engage in a bit of tail chasing. Note the opening for the camera mounted in the top lip of the air intake. This projects an image back to the ground station allowing the drone pilot to fly the Sabre during weapons testing.*

six years ago Northrop took over the contract."

In order to facilitate easy conversions, Northrop built a modern facility at nearby Inyokern Airport—a civilian facility that occasionally finds a Sabre in the pattern along with assorted light aircraft! Northrop sold this operation to the NSI Division of Mantech, but Northrop still provides the test pilots to check out the aircraft after they go through the conversion process.

Current contracts call for thirteen Sabres to be delivered per year. As of February 1989, 114 drones have been constructed. NSI does a thorough IRAN (Inspection and Repair As Necessary) and installs the drone gear. The Sabre then gets a couple of test flights to make sure everything is in top-notch order before delivery to the Navy.

China Lake is the last facility still rebuilding GE engines for the Sabres. NWC goes through the engines very carefully and brings the unit back to top military standards. General Electric also overhauls certain key components for the Navy.

Once completed, the drones are flown on very precise missions. "This isn't a Top Gun type of thing where you go out and dogfight with a drone and blow it out of the sky," said Wright. "All missions are flown very precisely, both on the drone's and attacker's part. We are here to collect the maximum amount of information. Most of the time, the missile has a telemetry warhead that transmits information on the

*Northrop chief test pilot Paul Metz positions QF–86F 807 close to the camera plane. This particular aircraft had served with the Japanese Self Defense Air Force before being withdrawn from service and returned to the United States.*

Next page

*Metz executes a steep break away from the camera plane. The discerning viewer will note the painted-over Japanese hinomaru insignias under the wing.*

function of the fuze, guidance system, etc. We gather lots of information on each flight. Sometimes the missile scores a direct hit on the drone but since it doesn't have a warhead, the drone stands some chance of surviving. I've recovered drones with big chunks of tail or wing missing. We rebuild them and they're ready for another mission. Sometimes the drone survives fifteen missions, sometimes it's destroyed on its first flight."

With supplies of convertible Sabres rapidly dwindling, the NWC may acquire 130 to 140 Sabres that are in storage with the Korean Air Force. These aircraft are all high-time machines and not in particularly good condition, and there is a distinct possibility these Sabres would be built up as "drone only" aircraft without the capability of having a real pilot.

As supplies of Sabres dwindle, the Navy's requirement for a viable drone will remain and over the next few years we will undoubtedly be seeing more and more QF–4 Phantom II conversions, many airframes of which are already in storage at China Lake.

There is a possibility that some of the left-over drone material may make its way to the civilian Sabre market but with around half a dozen civilian Sabres flying and several more under rebuild, we will have an active reminder of this most famous of all North American jet fighters for some years to come.

*Paul Metz displays the QF–86F against the wooded mountains near the Inyokern Airport where conversions are carried out. Unfortunately, few if any of these beautiful aircraft will survive the weapons testing role.*

# Chapter 8

# Fouga Magister

"Hotcakes! Selling like hotcakes. Yes sir, hotcakes."

The irrepressible Dean Martin (owner/operator and chief pilot of the Burlington, Vermont, based Warplanes Inc.) was tightly clutching a prospective customer by the elbow and giving him a quick walk-around of the "hotcake," a rather attractive Fouga Magister that was, obviously, for sale.

Warplanes Inc. is the purveyor of the exotic, esoteric and eclectic in former military flying machines and one of Martin's most successful aircraft has been the V-tailed Magister.

"Can't keep 'em on the ramp," stated Martin, a former farm boy that found his true calling in the sky. Warplanes Inc. has been directly responsible for adding dozens of the two-seat trainers to the American civil register, making the plane one of the most numerous of jet warbirds.

"Those ones from Finland went quick. Real quick," stated Martin to the possible customer. "Had to go to Israel. Worked a deal. Got 'em coming in," Martin continued in his clipped Yankee dialect. "Best two-seat jet value in the sky. Just get in an' go flying."

The Potez Air-Fouga CM.170 Magister, as the type was originally called, came about with a European requirement for an aircraft that could effectively train students to enter the new jet age. The Magister design went on to become one of the most successful of all European jets with over 1,000 examples built.

During late 1956, five French firms (Breguet, Dassault, Morane-Saulnier, Sud-Est Aviation and Ouest Aviation) formed a new company to take over the aircraft establishment of Establissements Fouga. Named Air-Fouga, this firm operated until mid 1958 when it was taken over by Potez. The main product of the company was the CM.170R which entered production for France, Belgium, the Netherlands, Finland, Austria and Germany. Clearly the CM.170R was an aircraft for Europe!

The Magister is a light two-seat trainer. A contract for three prototypes was signed on 27 June 1951 and the first flew on 23 July 1952. In June 1953, a pre-production order was placed for ten aircraft with the first of these flying on 7 July 1954. The first production Magister (Latin for "teacher" or "master") flew on 29 February 1956 and the plane went into full series production. Germany wanted 250 aircraft for its new Luftwaffe and purchased forty complete aircraft along with many sub-assemblies, and set up a production line in Germany to complete the rest. Belgium ordered forty-five aircraft for a joint Belgian/Dutch NATO training program.

License agreements were signed with Austria, Finland and Israel where Magisters were produced for training

*Owners of Fouga Magisters are employing a variety of creative paint schemes for their aircraft. N204DM is finished in a very attractive gloss black with silver trim and carries the name* Dog Whistle, *which is quite appropriate since the screech from the twin Turbomeca Marbore IIA turbojets is guaranteed to wake any dog within several miles of the airport.*

and attack missions. The Israelis found the Magister to be a particularly useful aircraft and, over the years, have modified their fleet to meet changing requirements. Israeli Magisters have seen more than their share of combat.

The Zephyr is a navalized variant of the Magister that was produced for France's Aeronavale. Modifications included catapult hook and holding strap, arrestor hook and two separate rearward sliding canopies to replace the Magister's upward hinged units. First flown on 31 July 1956, the type completed carrier qualifications and was used for air combat training, instrument flying instruction and training for carrier landing.

The CM.209 Super Magister, equipped with two Turbomeca Marbore VI turbojets of 1,058 lbs. thrust each, was first flown in mid 1960 and offered improved performance.

When Dean Martin imported his first Fougas, many pilots thought the little jet was rather strange looking with its low stance, V-tail and long tapered wing ending in tip tanks. The Magister is a bit different but is a rather elegant aircraft when compared to the USAF's Cessna T–37 trainer, which performs the same basic function and is fitted with license-built Marbores.

For many years, France's national aerobatic team used a fleet of Magisters and put on some incredible displays of flying. Accordingly, at least four Fouga owners are getting together to form a civilian aerobatic team that should be a big hit at the increasing

*Here's an unusual formation: Robb Satterfield flies wing, in the de Havilland Venom, on James Oliver and his Magister N903DM, a former Finnish machine imported by Dean Martin, over central California during August 1988. Oliver, an attorney, likes using the Fouga for some of his business trips since he can get to a client's location in short order without being at the mercy of the commercial airlines.*

*Israel has had a long and intimate association with the Magister—using the aircraft for training as well as ground attack. In Florida, John Silberman obtained CM.170 N5040N and painted the Fouga in camouflage with Israeli markings. Like all of Silberman's aircraft, the Fouga carries his own personal insignia of a black cat in a yellow circle. In military service the Magister has been used by France, Germany, Finland, Israel and a few Central American and African nations (usually in some form of mercenary operation). The Magister is capable of carrying two 7.5 mm machine guns in the nose and can carry small stores of bombs or light rockets under the wing.*

number of airshows in the United States.

The Magister offers twin-jet reliability, P–51 performance, jet fighter thrills and a comfortable environmen-

tally controlled cockpit. The engines, however, produce an ear-splitting shriek that will cause spectators to cover their ears while the Fouga taxis on the ramp (the same is true of the T–37). Also, the engines are somewhat sensitive and have to be handled according to the manual's instructions. They do not like rapid movements of the throttle and can flame out at altitude if mistreated. The Magister's high entry speeds and very clean airframe makes for very pleasant aerobatic maneuvers. The aircraft can even be spun if the tip tanks are empty, but a minimum of 4,000 ft. is required for recovery.

Dean Martin is looking forward to importing more Magisters once negotiations are complete with several other air forces, and we are sure these aircraft will quickly find buyers. For the reasonable acquisition price—in the $100,000 to $150,000 range depending on equipment—it's great fun.

Next page

*Landing light on, James Oliver shows off the very sleek frontal area of Magister N903DM. The CM.170 spans 37 ft. ¾ in., is 33 ft. 9½ in. long, and is 9 ft. 2¼ in. tall. With the two Marbore IIAs pumping out 880 lbs. of thrust each, the manual states the aircraft will hit 443 mph at 30,000 ft.*

Next page

*On the ramp at Mt. Hope, Hamilton, Canada, Magister N903DM has its canopies open to disperse the heat from an unusually warm day during June 1986. With the non-jettisonable tip tanks, the Magister has a range of 575 miles when operating at 30,000 ft.*

# Chapter 9

# Hawker Hunter

There's an ancient adage in aviation that proclaims, "If an aircraft looks right, then it'll fly right." Now perhaps that's a bit simplistic—and not overly accurate in this day of computer assisted flight controls that allow some of the most unlikely airframes to fly in a fairly convincing manner—but it is certainly a true statement when one regards the sublime lines of the graceful Hawker Hunter.

The Hunter was conceived as a replacement for the first-generation Gloster Meteor fighter. The Royal Air Force wanted an aircraft with plenty of performance and a heavy armament to serve as a daylight interceptor to counter the growing Soviet menace. Without waiting for official specifications to be issued, Hawker proceeded with design P.1067 which was presented on paper to the RAF during January 1948. The new plane was to weigh 12,000 lbs. and mount two of the new 30 mm Aden cannon. The intake for the jet would be in the nose, and the horizontal tail would be placed atop the vertical. As shown in the accompanying photographs, the design changed considerably before metal was cut.

Hawker decided to utilize the new Rolls-Royce AJ65 turbojet (which would later receive the name Avon) in two of the proposed three prototypes; the Armstrong-Siddeley Sapphire would be used in the third.

Wind tunnel tests showed that the horizontal stabilizer would function better if moved down on the vertical. The nose air intake was moved to the wing root to allow room for radar and other equipment in the nose. Also, the armament was increased to four 30

mm weapons installed in a clever pack that could be removed from the plane in just over a minute. A fresh gun pack complete with ammunition could then be quickly inserted, thus reducing sortie turnaround time by a significant amount.

Before the first flight, Hawker received orders to proceed with the planning for 200 of the new fighters to be powered by Avons—the RAF needed new fighters and needed them quickly.

The first P.1067 took to the air on 20 July 1951 from the RAF's testing base at Boscombe Down. Test pilot Neville Duke was at the controls of WB188 (the RAF serial) and was enthusiastic about the potential of the new fighter.

The first prototype did not have weapons and other production features but the second prototype, WB195, was up to production standards and carried the Aden cannons.

With all three prototypes flying, production was quickly introduced and the first Hunter Mk. 1 took to the air on 16 May 1953, an admirably short time from the prototype's first flight.

During testing it was determined that an air brake of some form was needed, so sleek was the Hunter's form that it was hard to slow down the aircraft. Some headscratching went on about where to place the air brake before it was finally decided to install

*Combat Jets Hunter was originally restored in Britain by Spencer Flack. The aircraft saw service with the Royal Danish Air Force before being surplused.*

the unit under the rear fuselage, the bulbous unit rather marring the otherwise near perfect lines.

The first twenty Hunter Mk. 1s were set aside for test work, and the first unit to receive the type was No. 43 Squadron. Only three squadrons would operate the Mk. 1 (the other two were No. 54 and No. 222) since the type was more of a transitional aircraft, and the majority of Mk. 1s were transferred to operational conversion units as newer variants became available.

Shortly after entering service, a teething problem arose with the Hunter. When the weapons were fired, the engine began to surge and sometimes quit or failed. This obviously was an unacceptable situation in a high-performance single-engine fighter. The engine was ingesting gases generated by the firing of the cannon and an altitude restriction was placed on the operation of the weapons until a fix could be devised.

This problem aside, the Hunter gained quick popularity among the pilots. The plane was very responsive, immensely strong and capable of gut-wrenching maneuvers (this was in the day before G-suits were completely reliable).

Hawker and the RAF decided to groom the first prototype, WB188, for a series of record flights. An Avon RA.7R engine with afterburning (7,130 lbs. thrust, 9,300 lbs. thrust with burner) was installed and the entire airframe was cleaned up and streamlined with a pointed nose and swept windscreen. Painted a glorious overall scarlet, Neville Duke set an absolute world three kilometer speed record of 727.6 mph on 7 September 1953. A few days later, Duke broke the 100 kilometer closed course record at 709.2 mph. It's interesting to note that this aircraft did

not feature the bulbous, drag-producing air brake but, rather, had small petal-style units mounted on each side of the rear fuselage.

The first definitive production variant of the Hunter was the Mk. 4, which enjoyed considerable success with the RAF and gained large production orders for the type. The Mk. 4 also featured the ability to carry underwing drop tanks and weapon stores, thus extending the range and capability of the fighter. The first Mk. 4 flew on 20 October 1954, and first deliveries were to No. 54 and No. 111 Squadrons.

In Germany, Mk. 4s began replacing Meteor Mk. 8s and de Havilland Venoms, giving the RAF a first-rate fighter to put up against the growing Warsaw Pact air forces. The first production group of Mk. 4s had the Avon 113 engine, but subsequent aircraft were fitted with Avon 115s which had been suitably reworked to counter engine surge during gun firing.

In operational training exercises, the Hunter's single-point refueling system and replaceable gun pack allowed sorties to turn around in as little as seven minutes. Experiments were undertaken with several Hunters to fit various underwing loads including high-velocity rockets and bombs. The Hunter turned out to be a particularly fine rocket and bomb launching platform, launching a new career for the fighter.

Production of the Hunter continued through a wide variety of subtypes that included side-by-side dual-control trainers and many export variants for foreign nations eager for a warplane with both fighter and ground-attack capabilities. It's interesting to note that all RAF day fighter squadrons in Europe had been equipped with Hunter Mk. 6s by 1958.

Today, the RAF and Royal Navy still operate a few Hunters in specialized roles, but the type is fast disappearing from British service. The Hunter flies on with several foreign air forces including Switzerland and Chile. The Swiss examples have been subjected to numerous updates over the

*Ed Schneider displays the beautiful planform of the Combat Jets Hunter. Currently, Hunters are still flying operationally with several air forces including those of Switzerland and Chile.*

years and, like other Swiss aircraft, are kept in exceedingly fine operational condition. The Swiss Hunters will probably continue to remain in front line service into the next century.

One of the first export customers to purchase the Hunter was Denmark. In July 1954, before the first RAF Mk. 4 was completed, Denmark placed an order for thirty aircraft similar to the Mk. 4 and designated them Mk. 51. Like the RAF aircraft, the original Avons were modified to overcome the surge problem during cannon firing. Operating with No. 724 Squadron at Aalborg, the planes gave particularly good service in NATO operations. In 1958, the Danes also took delivery of two T.Mk. 53 dual-control trainers that were similar to the RAF's T.7s and powered by Avon 122 engines.

When these aircraft were phased out of service in the early 1970s, some of the airframes found their way to Britain. The majority wound up in small museums courtesy of Hawker-Siddeley who had taken the planes in on trade, but several are now owned and flown by warbird enthusiasts in England and the United States.

One machine, Royal Danish Air Force E–403, was purchased by Al Letcher and transported to his base in Mojave, California. Letcher got the Mk. 51 back flying and the aircraft was assigned the civil registration N72602. Letcher enjoyed flying the plane and "booming" the area as he broke the sound barrier with the Hunter in a shallow dive. N72602 was then sold to Al Hansen who maintains the Hunter in flying condition at Mojave.

Another former Danish Hunter is currently undergoing restoration with Ed Stead in Bedford, New Hampshire.

*"Hunter flight break left now!" The Sabre and MiG belonging to Combat Jets break away from the all-scarlet Hunter. Three Hunters are currently airworthy in the United States while one further example is under rebuild to flying condition.*

*Al Letcher's Hunter Mk. 51 N72602 is seen at Mojave shortly after being rebuilt back to flying status. Spanning 33 ft. 8 in., 45 ft. 10½ in. long, and 13 ft. 2 in. high, the Mk. 51's top speed is Mach 0.93 at 36,000 ft.*

Former RDAF ET–271, this plane was obtained from the Booker Aircraft Museum in Britain in less-than-ideal shape.

Northern Lights Aircraft Inc. of Montgomery, Alabama, is currently flying a Hunter T.Mk. 7 registered as N576NL. The recently restored aircraft is part of Northern Lights' fleet which also includes CF–104D N104NL. Both aircraft are operated on research contracts and the Hunter gained a bit of fame when it was recently featured on a television commercial racing a Nissan automobile.

In Britain, the Hunter has also enjoyed a civilian life. A former Royal Netherlands Air Force T.Mk. 53 (N–307) was obtained by Denmark as ET–274 and when surplused went to Hawker-Siddeley's Dunsfold Aerodrome in Britain. The plane was restored to flying condition with the registration G-BOOM and is currently operated by

Jet Heritage at Hurn Airport in Bournemouth, England.

In 1977, British warbird collector Spencer Flack obtained a former RDAF Mk. 51 (E–418) and had the single-seat Hunter restored to beautiful flying condition as G-HUNT. Flown for the first time after restoration from Elstree Aerodrome on 20 March 1988, the Hunter was finished in Flack's "house" colors of overall scarlet—making for a magnificent sight. In 1981, the Hunter was sold to Mike Carlton. After Carlton's untimely death in an African plane crash, his fleet of vintage jets was dispersed and G-HUNT was sold to the Combat Jets Flying Museum based at Houston-Hobby Airport in Texas.

This Hunter was initially registered as N5097Z (now N611JR) and, like the rest of the Combat Jets collection, is maintained in perfect flying condition. Its glorious scarlet paint scheme has been retained (which honors Neville Duke's record-breaking flight in WB188) and it is a regular participant in American airshows.

It is possible that more Hunters may eventually find their way onto the American register (the two-seat variants are particularly valuable for research and flight test work). Until then, the American jet warbird community is fortunate to have three flying examples of what is arguably the most attractive of all British jet fighters.

*Chapter 10*

# Douglas Skyhawk

Without a doubt, the Douglas A–4 Skyhawk is one of the most effective naval attack aircraft ever built. The US Navy wanted a small attack aircraft that could carry a variety of weapons, including nuclear, to the target. Chief Engineer of Douglas Aircraft Ed Heinemann designed a small, low wing delta jet so compact it did not require folding wings for storage aboard the Navy's aircraft carriers.

The Navy liked what it saw and placed an order for twenty test machines on 13 June 1954. On 22 June 1954, the first XA4D–1 took to the air. Initially powered by a Wright J65–W–2 engine of 7,200 lbs. thrust, the aircraft was an immediate success. By August of that year, the first of 165 A4D–1s had been ordered and was equipped with the more powerful J65–W–4 of 7,700 lbs. thrust.

Variants of the Skyhawk, as the type was named, came fast and furious. The A4D–2 (542 built) first flew on 26 March 1956 and had inflight refueling capability along with other improvements, including the ability to carry two Bullpup missiles or a dozen Mk. 81 bombs of 300 lbs. each. The center fuselage rack could carry a Mk. 28 or Mk. 91 nuclear bomb.

The A4D–2N had limited all-weather capability and was fitted with APG–53A radar, first flying on 21 August 1958. Douglas built 638 –2Ns. The next variant was the A4D–5 with the Pratt & Whitney J52–P–6A of 8,500 lbs. thrust. Douglas built 498 of these aircraft which now carried the designation A–4E to conform with the new tri-service designation system introduced in the early 1960s. The last A–4E was delivered in April 1966 and could carry 9,155 lbs. of underwing weapons.

The A–4F was the last new Navy production variant of the attack plane. First flown on 31 August 1966, the F was powered by a P&W J52–P–8A of 9,300 lbs. thrust. The Marines finally got their own variant, the A–4M, which first flew on 10 April 1970 and had an updated engine, larger canopy, drag chute, larger ammunition load and other items required for the Marine ground support mission. The final M was delivered on 27 February 1979 and the closing of the line saw a total of 2,960 Skyhawks built in twenty-five years of continuous production.

One very popular variant was the dual-control Skyhawk trainer. The first such example, a TA–4F, flew on 30 June 1965 and retained the majority of the attack capability of the single-seater. By 1969, delivery started on the TA–4J and, in all, 555 trainers were eventually built.

Rebuilt Skyhawks also enjoyed a healthy career. Rebuilt A–4Bs for Argentina became A–4Ps and Qs. New Australian Navy craft were A–4Gs. New

*Guy Neeley displays the Skyhawk's small frontal area in this head-on view. The A–4A spans a mere 27 ft. 6 in., is 39 ft. 4 in. long, and stands 15 ft. 2 in. tall.*

Next page
*Guy Neeley was killed and N444V completely destroyed on 4 June 1987 when the aircraft rolled into the ground during a low pass for cameras filming a commercial.*

Zealand got A–4Ks; Kuwait, A–4KUs; Singapore, A–4Ss; Israel, A–4Hs and A–4Ns; and so on. Israel is a major user of the Skyhawk and heavy losses of the type during the Egyptian invasion of 1969 caused US Navy and Marine aircraft to be flown directly to Israel as replacements. Currently, Singapore builds a highly modified variant of the A–4 which it hopes to sell to other countries.

During the Vietnam War, Navy and Marine Skyhawks racked up countless missions. Argentina used the Skyhawk to advantage during the Falklands/Malvinas War and, as mentioned, the Israeli Skyhawks have seen plenty of action. With the constant rebuilding of Skyhawks and losses in combat, few of these excellent machines have been made available to the civilian market.

The few flying Skyhawks currently on the civil register have been built up from hulks acquired from junkyards and displays. During the late 1970s, Pascal Mahvi acquired an early A–4A that had been discarded as a gate guardian. The plane was transported to Chino, California, and left in the care of Unlimited Aircraft Ltd. Rebuilt over four years, many improvements and an upgraded engine were added to the lightweight A–4A airframe. Registered as N444AV to Advanced Aero Enterprises, this beautiful aircraft did not enjoy a long flying life. While flying for a television commercial near California City, California, experienced A–4 pilot Guy Neeley was killed after the plane appeared to roll while flying

*A–4A N444V (BuNo 14219) was beautifully restored from a hulk by Unlimited Aircraft Ltd. at Chino Airport. Owned by Aeronautical Test Vehicles, the plane was used for flight test and film work. The A–4A (which featured an upgraded engine and systems) is accompanied by Canadair Silver Star N133AT. Few Skyhawks have been placed on the civil register because of the worldwide demand for the type.*

quite low to the ground. The accident happened on 4 June 1987 and was a blow to the warbird community.

At Flight Systems' Mojave, California, base three Skyhawks were acquired on bailment from the Navy: A–4C N401FS (BuNo 148571, ex N53996), A–4L N402FS (BuNo 149516) and A–4L N403FS (BuNo 150586). Flight Systems used these aircraft for a variety of test programs before returning the planes to the military after completion of the test work. N402FS was operated by Flight Systems for the longest period of time, between 1977 and 1984; N401FS is now with the Pima Air Museum in Tucson, Arizona.

At Addison, Texas, Dave Straight's Sierra Hotel Aviation has completed a beautiful restoration of Skyhawk N21NB which is finished in Royal New Zealand Air Force aggressor colors. N21NB is flown regularly and has appeared in several advertisements and commercials.

Painted in very authentic Vietnam War colors, A–4B BuNo 142112 is one of Combat Jets Flying Museum's newest airworthy jets. Registered N3E, the Skyhawk is a very popular airshow performer.

As one can see, the total civilian Skyhawk population is small but this will probably change as John Dilley in Indiana and Tom Reilley in Florida have plans to restore several Skyhawks for civilian use. Also, a few air forces are beginning to phase out their A–4s and there's a good chance some of these planes will return to the United States and civilian ownership.

*N403FS was one of three civil-registered Skyhawks operated by Flight Systems for test programs. On completion of the work, the aircraft were returned to the Navy. The A–4L here is at Mojave in January 1980.*

# Chapter 11

# Saab Draken

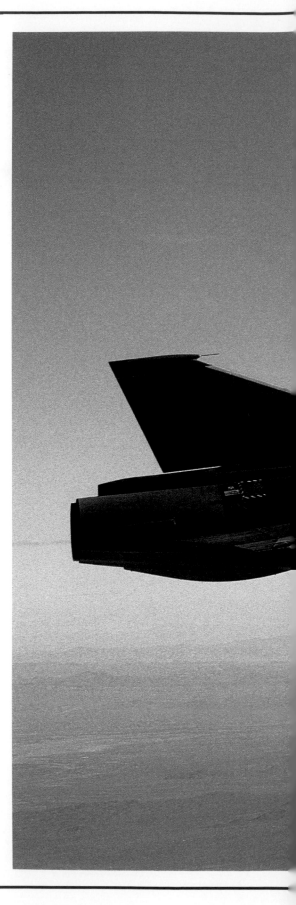

The Mustang's Merlin was humming along at sixty inches of manifold pressure, filling the cramped cockpit with an ungodly roar that only a Rolls-Royce V–12 motor can. We were rapidly scanning the sky for our intended target—without luck. Radio transmission was sketchy at best.

"Can't read you, Skip," said Matt Jackson who was up front—handling the driving chores. I was in the excuse for a back seat that makes virtually all surviving flyable Mustangs into two-seaters. We were at 12,000 feet above Palmdale Airport (or, to those of you with a more militaristic bent, USAF Plant 42)—home of the Rockwell B–1B and Northrop B–2 Stealth Bomber. We finally spotted our target—coming head on at a closing speed of well over 1,000 mph.

"Gotcha, Mustang," said Skip Holm's disembodied voice over the rough intercom. The Saab J35F–2 Draken (Swedish for Dragon—they have a hard time living down all that Viking stuff) zeroed-in on the P–51D and swept past in fairly close proximity, Skip racking the double-delta jet in a tight turn—or at least as tight as a Mach 2 double-delta can turn.

The morning sun was rising over Mt. Baldy as we headed on our easterly course, and now Skip was facing directly into the sun, as we were.

The magnificent visibility afforded by the bubble canopy on the Mustang allowed me to watch all these maneuvers with just the slightest turn of the head.

"Ah, Mustang lead—I can't see you, I'm looking right into the sun."

"Come on, Skip," said a rather exasperated Jackson. "You're supposed to be a fighter pilot. We're at your 12 o'clock high. Remember that? They taught it to you in the Air Force."

"Roger that," said Skip. "I'm still looking."

Now, even though I don't like to, I have to stick up for Skip because he was flying a new aircraft for the first time and had been airborne for only a couple of minutes. Even worse, up to a few days previously, Skip didn't even know what a Draken was!

We had been out at Mojave Airport—situated in California's high desert—in November 1989 to test the Gloster Meteor. Now, I'm completely convinced that Skip Holm can fly just about anything with—or without—wings but he does have a hard time with aircraft identification.

"That's a Gloster Meteor, Skip," I said while pointing to the camouflaged lump squatting at a sinister angle on the Mojave ramp.

"Oh, that's a Meteor," said Skip in a burst of acuity. "Looks nice."

Well, Skip thinks that any airplane looks nice—whether it's a Cessna 150 or a B–2 Stealth Bomber.

"Yeah, Skip—looks great. Know anything about Meteors?"

*N543J is shown airborne over the Mojave Desert. In military service, this variant of the Draken is normally equipped with one 30 mm Aden cannon. When the Draken entered service, the only other comparable all-weather double Mach interceptor was the Convair F-106 Delta Dart.*

"I think it's made in England," said Skip.

From that point the conversation went downhill.

While the Meteor was being serviced for Skip's flight, I took him into Al Hansen's large hangar—a space packed with aeronautical treasures. Taking up one corner of the facility was the ultra-sleek form of the Saab Draken.

"Know what that is Skip?" I asked, pointing at the J35F.

"Er, em, uh," he said as he rubbed his chin—steely blue eyes boring into the dull olive drab camouflage of the former Swedish Air Force jet.

"Is it some form of Mirage?" queried our ace pilot.

"No."

"How about one of those British Lightnings?"

"No. Come on, Skip! It's a contemporary fighter. When you were flying in the USAF, you could have encountered one of these things on a daily basis in a NATO war situation, you've gotta know what it is!"

"How about one of those older MiGs?"

"No! You used to have a car made by the same company."

"It's a Saab!" exclaimed our test pilot.

"Right! What flavor?"

"Is that important?"

"Like I said, you might have to make a life or death decision in a war. What would you do?"

"Shoot it down," said Skip. End of conversation.

*As befits a Mach 2 aircraft, the Draken is sleek and attractive from any angle. A world-class fighter when it was developed in the 1950s, the Draken remains a potent weapon through the use of many improvements and updates over the course of its service life. As of this writing, three Drakens are in the United States. Two of the fighters are owned by Bill Marizan while the third, which had been imported by Dean Martin, had just been sold to a new owner.*

111

*This rear view of N543J (Royal Swedish Air Force serial number 35543) shows off the massive afterburner for the RM6C powerplant. The two small tailwheels are also clearly visible. With 17,262 lbs. of thrust, the J35F can reach 1,320 mph at 36,000 ft. Initial rate of climb is 35,500 feet per minute. The span of the fighter is only 30 ft. 10 in., while the length is 50 ft. 10 in.*

The Saab J35 Draken is certainly one of the most distinctive shapes in the current jet warbird movement. The J35 is, however, also an actively serving warplane with the air forces of Sweden,

Denmark, Finland and Austria. The Saab J35 is a combination of bold, innovative design blended with sparkling performance.

After the conclusion of World War II, Sweden developed a policy of creating aircraft for its air force and suited to Sweden's own particular needs. The rapid escalation of the Cold War and the development of advanced bombers by Sweden's neighbor, the Soviet Union, led to a certain amount of worry. Saab had already created the J32 Lansen, an afterburning all-weather fighter that was equal to anything being flown by the Allies. But the Lansen, like the other fighters, was not capable of meeting and defeat-

ing what was perceived as the new threat: Soviet bombers capable of fighting their way into the target at Mach 0.9 plus and at high altitudes.

It fell to Saab engineers to create a plane that would not drain Swedish resources, be capable of operating from existing Swedish airbases without major base modification, and be available in a reasonable amount of time. Also, the top speed would obviously have to be very well in excess of Mach 1 to enable adequate kill time.

At this point, 1949, supersonic flight was a reality but it was a discipline inhabited only by exotic rocket and research aircraft. Certainly, considerable work was being done by the major powers in developing supersonic fighters but it fell to little Sweden to set the pace by developing a fighter that was not only radical in performance capabilities but also in appearance.

The supersonic aircraft built up to that time were test vehicles with incredibly small wings, little maneuvering capability and extremely limited fuel stocks with absolutely no combat potential. The Swedes rejected any sort of then-conventional layout and opted for an aircraft with an amazing seventy-degree leading edge sweep. In fact, the first paper designs looked almost like an advanced arrowhead: virtually a flying double-delta wing.

It was decided to build a small working prototype called the Saab 210 to test the various theories. One of the problems of any fighter is fuel. With jet fighters this problem compounds because of the thirsty powerplant. By utilizing a double-delta configuration, the Swedes could load the inboard portion of the delta with fuel while the much thinner outboard portion would enable the supersonic speeds desired.

The 210 test bed was flown on 21 January 1952 and its appearance and performance startled the world's aviation press. Simply constructed and utilizing an Armstrong-Siddeley Adder for power, the 210 clipped along at over 400 mph and proved the double-delta concept.

For the full-size J35 prototype, the afterburning Svenska Flygmotor RM5 was developed from the Rolls-Royce Avon. Orders for three prototypes were received in mid 1953 and the first flight was made on 25 October 1955—a surprisingly short time considering the construction and design problems that had to be overcome.

Even though the prototypes had flown, there was much work to be done. Certain portions of the aircraft had to be redesigned to give increased structural strength while the prototype's engine was replaced with the now-ready RM65B with Type 65 afterburner. Except for the prototype USAF Convair F–106, the Draken, at this point, had the whole all-weather supersonic interceptor market to itself.

First operational deliveries took place in 1960 and problems were discovered with control sensitivity that result in some damaged Drakens. However, once in service the Draken proved to be a superior aircraft—exceeding performance and flying hours versus maintenance hours expectations.

As with virtually all their other modern combat aircraft, the Swedes developed the basic J35 design to perform a variety of combat missions. The J35A featured an early CFS Cyrano radar, a Lear autopilot and Saab S6 fire control. Armament consisted of two Aden M55 30 mm cannon buried in the inboard delta wing.

Developments and improvements on the basic design have continued throughout the aircraft's service life. A new afterburner, the Type 66, was installed starting in late 1960 and resulted in a longer rear fuselage. A drag chute was added along with two small wheels to protect the rear fuselage in place of the skid which prevented damage in case of an extreme tail down landing. Sidewinders and appropriate fire control systems came along shortly thereafter. The first of the two-seat Drakens, the J35C, was soon operating alongside the single-seaters.

The J35B had a longer rear fuselage, direct tie-in with the nationwide STRIL 60 air defense network, improved fire control and ability to carry rocket pods or small bombs.

The J35D was equipped with the RB.146 engine mated to an improved afterburner resulting in the RM6C—the most powerful of all Avon variants. This powerplant gave the J35D a Mach 2 speed combined with a near 50,000 foot per minute (fpm) rate of climb. Deliveries of the J35D began in 1963.

The S35E was also first flown in 1963 and was basically a J35D equipped with a camera nose capable of carrying five cameras. Two more cameras were installed in the area once occupied by the cannons. This aircraft gave the Swedish Air Force an advanced recon capability beyond most other nations.

The most important of all Draken variants is the J35F which is based on a greatly modified J35D airframe. Saab engineers took a J35D apart and discovered various means of cramming more gear into an already very full space. The extremely powerful PS–01 radar was installed and it would not be equalled in Europe until the arrival of the American F–14 Tomcat and F–15 Eagle, many years later. A distinctive Hughes infrared (IR) sensor was added under the nose and the IR and radar fed the S7B fire control system. Major improvements to other systems, including autopilot, ejection seat, instruments, canopy and data link, resulted in a very impressive fighter.

Armament for the J35F was upgraded to carry four modified versions of the Hughes Falcon air-to-air missile (AAM), two for radar homing work (RB27) and two for infrared homing (RB28). One cannon was eliminated for additional electronics room. The J35F was also capable of toting eleven external pylons for weapons or additional fuel tanks. Somehow, the Saab engineers managed to increase the internal fuel to 880 gallons— an increase of over forty percent when compared to earlier variants.

It was with this variant that Saab scored export sales successes to Finland, Denmark and Austria. The J35F gave the Swedes a very potent weapon with which to counter possible Soviet aggression and the Soviets, having had bad experiences in Scandanavia during the Winter War, realized this fact.

The Draken is still being modified to meet the changing demands of defending Swedish airspace; approximately sixty J35Fs are being upgraded to J35J configuration.

After the 35 series, Saab went on to develop the mighty Saab 37 Viggen (Thunderbolt) which went on to become a modern combat aircraft success story that was built in a number of variants to perform a variety of missions much like the Draken. The Saab 35 and 37 currently operate alongside

each other and give Sweden a very powerful air force.

Unfortunately, troubles arose with the new consortium-developed JAS–39 Gripen (Griffon). The high-technology Gripen was developed, once again, to fulfill several roles, but its advanced design and computer software led to many delays and the disastrous and widely publicized crash of the prototype after just a few test flights had been undertaken. The Gripen was designed to replace the majority of the Draken fleet along with some of the early Viggens, but the fact that the entire Gripen program has been put considerably behind schedule has caused the Swedish Air Force to retain the Draken fleet.

This retention has caused Bill Marizan, owner of J35F–2 N543J, a bit of a problem. A few years back, Marizan worked out a complex deal with the Swedish Air Force Museum that would see four Drakens travel to the United States in return for an ultra-rare de Havilland Mosquito. The Swedes had flown Mosquitos and needed an example for their expanding Air Force Museum. Since the Drakens were going out of service, the trade was quite favorable. Two single-seaters and two two-seaters were to be sent to the United States in return for the Mosquito. Because of the problems with the Gripen, only the two single-seaters have arrived, while the Draken force has had its service life extended.

Marizan hopes to obtain the remaining aircraft in order to start a flight test business. The Draken, after being licensed by the FAA, has participated in several test contracts where its high speed is of use.

Aircraft of this category fit well into the civilian flight test market. Many companies are eager to flight test their hardware, whether it be electronic systems, weapons systems or other equipment that needs to be hauled aloft by military type aircraft for testing. Several other forms of high-performance jet warbirds are being used in flight test work. A two-seat Draken would be of even greater use.

And what of Skip Holm's flight in the Draken? Actually, everything went pretty smoothly and he delivered the aircraft to Tucson, Arizona, where it was used in the new film *Wings of the Apache*—sort of a US Army *Top Gun* that sees Army McDonnell Douglas AH–64 Apache attack helicopters pitted against an evil drug lord. It just so happens that the drug lord has an air force and its star member is an all-black Draken with "just say yes to drugs" painted in Spanish on its flanks!

Skip Holm did some pretty exciting flying in the film, dogfighting with Apaches and making low-level attacks on various film sets. One "small" problem cropped up when the film makers set off a large explosive charge directly in front of the Draken's flight path, rather than behind the plane as called for in the script.

"It was kinda like going Downtown again," said Skip—referring to a previous life flying F–105s into Hanoi. "Those rocks and other debris hitting the plane sounded just like small arms fire."

The premature explosion did damage the Draken, ripping some healthy chunks out of the leading edge of the left wing and cracking the canopy.

"If some of those rocks had been ingested into the engine then Skip would have had to use the ejection seat," said Bill Marizan. "At that altitude, it would have been all over."

"Seems those Hollywood guys wanted me as bad as the North Vietnamese," commented Skip.

*The J35F's unique double-delta wing planform is well portrayed in this view of the powerful fighter. This type of wing allows for fuel and armament storage in the thicker inner portions while the thin outer portions allow for high Mach numbers.*

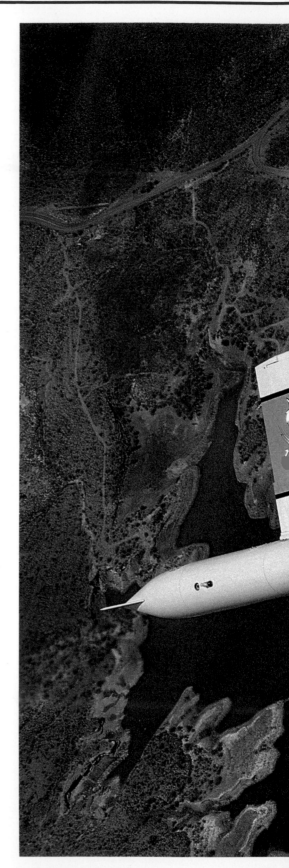

# Chapter 12

# Temco Pinto

Aviation is fraught with curious coincidences. One episode of unusual juxtaposition is how a jet trainer that was a complete failure for the United States Navy turned into a very desirable civilian aircraft.

During the 1950s, the armed forces of the United States were going through some dramatic changes. The jet warplane was firmly established but the pilot training syllabus still relied on the tried-and-true method of letting the fledgling aviator win his wings on propeller-driven trainers that had little or no relationship with the new jet warriors. To compound the difficulties, the venerable AT-6 Texan was still in service (although being phased out in large numbers) and while it is true that a student taught in a Texan can fly just about anything, the day of the tail wheel had been completely eclipsed by aircraft with tricycle landing gear.

The military realized new training aircraft were needed to teach the fine art of flying jets. There were, however, two schools of thought; those wanting to retain piston engine planes of new design and those desiring to create an all-jet training program. Jets aren't cheap, but the proponents of the all-jet program reasoned that the number of training hours could be reduced by the student being immediately introduced to the world of turbojet power.

Several proposals were submitted to the military for an all-jet training program and the plane that caught the US Navy's attention was the Temco TT-1 (an aircraft that would later gain the name Pinto). Temco was a small company located near Dallas, Texas, whose aviation manufacturing exper-

tise had included subcomponents, the TF-51D Mustang (a limited production conversion that turned the North American fighter into a dual control trainer) and the Swift (a small two-seat general aviation aircraft). Temco went on to become the T in the huge industrial conglomerate Ling, Temco and Vought (LTV).

Temco went so far as to construct a privately funded, civil-registered prototype to display to Navy officials. The small tandem-seat trainer was a graceful looking machine that comprised a central fuselage "pod" for crew and engine, a slim tail boom that carried a conventional tail and a straight wing that housed the main landing gear. The prototype made its first flight on 26 March 1956 and was powered by a Continental J69 turbojet that offered 920 lbs. of static thrust.

The Navy had doubts about an all-jet training program but the little Temco looked like a viable alternative since it was fairly cheap to produce and

*Chris Hall was also responsible for the conversion of Mike Dillon's N7752A to Super Pinto status. The tip tanks on Dillon's craft are from a Mitsubishi MU-2 and contribute to the plane's 250 gallon fuel capacity. At full throttle, the CJ-610 will eat up the fuel load in between 20 and 40 minutes depending on altitude. At a cross-country economy cruise of 325 knots at between 29,000 to 31,000 feet, Dillon figures the Pinto will get a still-air range of 600 nautical miles. The Pinto's original fuel capacity of 124 gallons was barely adequate for pattern work.*

*This Paulson Super Pinto has a more conventional tail unit installed and is shown in October 1974, painted in camouflage colors. The entire program was eventually sold but the Super Pinto prototype was destroyed in a crash and the plans for production were dropped.*

would provide an important role in transition training.

Several aviation reference sources disagree as to how many Pintos were procured by the Navy for its limited test program. The Navy decided to have a small batch of the planes built and then assigned to a training unit to see how they performed in creating aviators with "wings of gold." Some sources list fourteen as being ordered, others say thirteen which may simply refer to military machines and exclude the civil-registered prototype which differed in a number of respects from the production aircraft.

Of the number ordered, the Navy apparently only took actual delivery of ten Pintos (what happened to the remaining aircraft is a bit of a mystery)

and these machines were to go head-to-head with the new T–34 Mentor 225 hp piston-engine trainer being built by Beech for the Navy and Air Force.

The TT–1s entered service during late 1957 and were utilized to train two cycles of Naval Aviation cadets. Unfortunately, the program did not proceed smoothly. At Patuxent River Naval Air Station, Maryland, where the Navy does the majority of its aircraft testing, a test pilot had taken a Pinto up for spin trials. The test pilot started with three turn spins to the left and right with in-spin aileron and neutral aileron. This was simply a standard test procedure for any new aircraft capable of spinning. The pilot then tried out-spin aileron and suddenly found himself in deep trouble. The Pinto would not recover from the spin and the test pilot had no choice but to parachute to safety. The TT–1 was destroyed.

Another Pinto was destroyed during the training program when a cadet was doing touch-and-goes. Water on the runway was splashed by the nose gear into the low-slung air intakes and the engine flamed out when the Pinto

was about two-thirds down the runway while the pilot was rotating. With power gone and wet, ineffective brakes, the Pinto rolled off the end of the runway and over a cliff, killing the student.

Even though the Pinto seemed to perform its desired role, the Navy opted for the Beech T–34 because it was cheaper to obtain and operate. The surviving Pintos were sent to the Navy's vast storage yard at NAS Litchfield Park, Arizona, where they went into long-term storage with an average of just 600 hours on each airframe.

Four of the Pintos were eventually transferred to a California technical school where they would be used to train A&P mechanics in the fine art of jet maintenance. The remaining five planes were put up for sale.

Several individuals expressed interest in obtaining the machines but all the Pintos were purchased by Allied Aircraft, an aircraft salvage company. Allied did not want to scrap the planes, and instead resold them to individuals. The aircraft were probably obtained from the Navy for a few thousand dollars apiece and resold for a tidy profit;

118

even so, that price would still be considered very reasonable by the standards of today's warbird prices.

Several of the Pintos were flown to Van Nuys, California, where their Navy yellow training paint was stripped off and civilian schemes applied. Under the Navy paint, the aluminum skin was in fine condition, further illustration of just how little the trainers had been used.

Two of the Pintos were acquired by aviation entrepreneur Al Paulson who, at the time, was president of American Jet Industries. The other three went to various individuals. Paulson also managed to obtain the civil-registered prototype which apparently had been in storage in Texas.

As mentioned, the TT-1 was powered by a GE J69-T-9 engine which was a French Turbomeca Marbore built under license. This engine also powered the USAF's Cessna T-37 "Tweety Bird" trainer (which used two such powerplants). In its original form, the Pinto was distinctly underpowered.

Paulson felt that the Pinto could have a new military future if a new

engine and other modifications were added to the airframe. He set about to acquire the manufacturing rights for the plane and then gutted the original engine and systems out of one of his aircraft. In place of the J69, Paulson installed a GE CJ-610-6 that pumped out 2,950 lbs. of static thrust—quite an improvement over the original 920 lb. thrust unit! This engine was readily available since it was used in the Learjet 24 and the Northrop T-38 Talon (which used it in the afterburning J85 variant).

In order to install the engine, Paulson had to move the powerplant a foot farther aft than the J69 and extend the tail boom by eighteen inches. Also, 200 lbs. of lead had to be bolted in the nose to get the center of gravity back to a reasonable location. As the plane developed, Paulson added further improvements including tip tanks, a larger swept vertical tail and an exhaust attenuator. Dubbed the Super Pinto, the aircraft now offered sparkling performance and was flown for an *Air Progress* magazine pilot report by writer Mike Dillon, a TWA copilot who was

*Bob Lazier's Super Pinto was divided into 65 boxes of parts when he purchased the aircraft. Thousands of man-hours later, Chris Hall created this beautiful aircraft for Lazier. N4486L is equipped with a CJ-610 engine and is fitted with wingtip tanks from a Cessna 310.*

more than impressed by the Super Pinto's hot performance.

Paulson campaigned the Super Pinto at various airshows and aviation displays, looking for a production order. Over a period of several years, the Super Pinto was further refined and its overall yellow paint scheme gave way to a more militaristic camouflage.

Finally, the entire program was sold to the Philippines—licensing rights, the Super Pinto and the TT-1 prototype. The Filipinos hoped to build and export the plane as the Cali but the Super Pinto was soon destroyed in a crash that claimed the life of a high-ranking PAF officer and the pro-

*Developed for a possible US Navy requirement for an all-jet training fleet, the Temco TT-1 Pinto was a limited production aircraft that was not developed once the Navy standardized on the Beech T-34B Mentor for primary training. One of the nicest of the surviving TT-1s is Mike Dillon's Super Pinto N7752A.*

gram was dropped. A recent visitor to the island nation reported that the disassembled prototype was languishing in a hangar in rather poor condition, but there is a good chance that this machine will eventually return to the States for rebuild.

Another Pinto admirer was Frank Guzman who obtained two Pintos

shortly after Paulson acquired his. Guzman also undertook an engine change but in a different manner than American Jet's Super Pinto. Guzman modified the internal contours of the fuselage ring spar to allow the installation of the CJ-610 without changing the center of gravity.

Apparently not caring for the wingtip tank installation on the Super Pinto, Guzman made his wing wet—meaning that the entire wing structure was used for a fuel tank. He then had the wing sealed with fiberglass to ensure smoothness (and to keep the fuel in!). Guzman liked the final result and he carried out the same modification on his second Pinto.

Guzman then decided to increase the capabilities of his first Pinto and

began an extensive modification program that would see the fuselage modified to hold Mitsubishi MU-2 landing gear while the wing wheelwells were sealed over to hold another 100 gallons of Jet A. While this project was under way, Guzman was murdered in Miami, Florida. This Pinto is now being rebuilt to flyable condition.

In the mid 1970s, aviation businessman Steve Snyder obtained Pinto serial number 13 which was converted to a Guzman-style Super Pinto. Snyder still has the plane and has been flying a Pinto longer than any other owner. He calls the plane his "magic carpet." Quite the Pinto enthusiast, Snyder says, "If there ever was an affordable jet, this is it. It's the one materialistic thing in my life that I just have to have!" Snyder regularly flies his Super Pinto and attends many East Coast airshows with the high-performance aircraft. "It'll get off the ground in a thousand feet and stop in less than 2,000," he states.

Another Pinto owner is Bob Lazier who found his aircraft in a Salisbury, Maryland, salvage yard a dozen years ago. Buying the plane before he had a pilot's license, Lazier was a bit daunted when he found that the aircraft was basically a pile of parts. Lazier hired Chris Hall to rebuild the aircraft even though Hall had minimal aircraft experience. He was, however, a skilled craftsman and working for Lazier on other projects when Lazier purchased the craft.

The Pinto was basically divided into sixty-five boxes of parts and 575 sheets of plans, each 32 in. wide and 13 ft. long. Chris took the whole mess and trucked it to his shop at Vail, Colorado, where he started to put the Pinto together.

One of the first things Hall did was build a wooden mockup of the fuselage bulkheads, and then designed the new ductwork for the engine on this frame. He had to master a number of aeronautical skills for aircraft sheet metal work, fiberglass, aerodynamics and jet engine systems. The final result was so perfect that all the bits and pieces fitted together with no problem. It took four years.

The work on this aircraft led Hall to open a jet restoration and modification business in Vail, which led to work on three more Pintos.

Aircraft collector Mike Coutches in Hayward, California, had purchased the four Pintos that had gone to the technical school. Mike Dillon, who was by then a very successful businessman, still remembers doing that pilot report on the Super Pinto back in the late 1960s.

Dillon had gotten away from aviation a bit since he quit his job at TWA and opened Dillon Precision Industries. Based at Scottsdale, Arizona, Dillon was able to get a first-hand look at Lazier's Pinto. "It just seemed that the airplane with the CJ–610 engine was an ideal combination," recalled Dillon. "I started looking for a Pinto in 1985 and found one in Akron, Ohio. It had been hangared for sixteen years but had done very little flying. The owner said the plane was in pretty good condition and the price was $150,000 and he was not going to haggle. I immediately bought the Pinto."

Dillon went to Akron with Chris Hall and spent six days getting the Pinto ready for its ferry flight to Scottsdale. With friend Dave Clinton aboard, the ferry flight took three days—mainly because of problems with the hydraulic system. Once back at Scottsdale, Dillon turned the plane over to Hall for conversion to Super Pinto status. The resulting restoration won the 1988 Oshkosh trophy for Best Jet, and Chris Hall picked up the Silver Wrench award for excellence in restoration.

Dillon uses the Pinto for pleasure and business and appreciates the aircraft's sparkling performance. "I wouldn't trade it for an F–15," he states.

There are currently six Pinto airframes registered, with four of them flying—all in Super Pinto configuration. The Super Pinto is a limited production item, and it is such an excellent performing aircraft that it is doubtful any will be showing up on the pages of *Trade A Plane* in the foreseeable future.

# Chapter 13

# Northrop Talon

In 1984, Van Nuys Airport, located in the middle of Los Angeles' sprawling San Fernando Valley, became home to an aircraft with a unique pedigree: The first civilian owned and operated Northrop T–38A supersonic trainer.

During the 1950s, the USAF's operational fighters and some bombers were designed with supersonic capabilities. In order to keep pilot training on a par with these new machines, the USAF initiated plans to create the first supersonic trainer.

Northrop has always had a reputation for creativity and, in 1954, the company began a study to define a new, lightweight and inexpensive fighter aircraft that would conform to the needs of European and Asian countries that required high performance but could not afford the price of the front line fighters being built at that time.

The new design was called the N–156 and employed an airframe with a small wing and two efficient engines with afterburners. Called the Freedom Fighter, the design would evolve into the very successful F–5 series of combat aircraft.

The USAF was, of course, interested in this new warplane—not as a combat aircraft but as a possible trainer. Accordingly, Northrop advanced a modified version of the design called the N–156T to the USAF for

*This view of N683TC draws attention to the Talon's area ruled fuselage, essential for allowing the dual-control trainer to easily pass through the sound barrier.*

approval. Keeping the same basic layout, the N–156T was equipped with dual controls and configured to meet USAF training requirements. In December 1956, the USAF cautiously ordered three prototypes; this was upgraded to seven prototypes and one static test airframe in June 1958.

Designated YT–38, the new aircraft was unlike any other USAF trainer with its twin afterburners, tiny wing and area-ruled fuselage. Lew Nelson took the first aircraft, serial number 58–1191, aloft from the Edwards AFB California, runway on 10 April 1959. The first and second prototypes were not capable of exploring the design's full potential since they were fitted with non-afterburning General Electric YJ85–GE–1s. The new engines were available for the remainder of the YT–38 order and the YJ85–GE–5 with afterburning offered 3,600 lbs. thrust each (production aircraft would be fitted with J85–GE–5As of 3,850 lbs. thrust each with afterburning). Nelson was pleased with the new prototype, stating, "The T–38 is a clean airplane. The cleanest first flight in my experience—and the first with no squawks."

The USAF, being rather cautious, ordered thirteen T–38As with fiscal 1959 funds while the test program was being carried out. The first production aircraft, serial number 59–1594, made its first flight during May 1960 and the test program was completed by February 1961, one month ahead of schedule, after a staggering 2,000 flights.

The USAF accepted its first T–38A, now named Talon, on 17 March 1961 at Randolph AFB, Texas, with the 3510th Flight Training Wing. With

such a high-performance aircraft—top speed is 805 mph at 36,000 ft.—a new training syllabus was created to transition students from the lower-powered Cessna T–37s to the new "pocket rocket."

During this time period, America was responsible for a majority of the training for the new Luftwaffe. Most of this training was carried out in Texas and Arizona, the clear skies and excellent flying weather being just what the fledgling German aviators needed, especially when compared to the usually glum weather over the Continent. Since the Luftwaffe was beginning to operate high-performance warplanes, including the Starfighter, the Federal Republic of Germany announced it would purchase forty-six Talons for its student pilot program. These aircraft retained full USAF markings and training colors and were based at Sheppard AFB in Texas beginning in 1966.

Orders for the Talon increased and by the time the production line closed in January 1972, Northrop had built 1,187 T–38As. The Talon was employed by other users besides the Air Force, including the Navy which bought five T–38As in 1969 for the Navy Test Pilot School at Patuxent River, Maryland. NASA has also operated the Talon using the aircraft for everything from astronaut training and recurrency to high-speed transportation. In fact, NASA now operates the *first* production Talon, having obtained the aircraft in 1989.

This particular Talon was delivered to the USAF at Edwards AFB and served in the T–38 test program. The Talon then went on to a variety of mis-

Previous page
*Chuck Thornton's sleek Northrop T–38A Talon is seen against the rugged and harsh landscape of the Mojave Desert. The Talon is employed for a variety of uses to earn its keep, having done everything from being leased to Northrop for test work to being highly visible in commercials and film work.*

sions, such as chase plane on the C–141 StarLifter program. In the late 1960s, it served with a small USAF detachment at Los Angeles International Airport, providing flight support for the Air Force Manned Orbiting Laboratory Plan.

By 1974, the Talon was transferred to the Navy at NAS Miramar, San Diego, where it flew in the Navy's TOPGUN air combat training program. At Miramar, the Talon and its pilots imitated Soviet fighter aircraft, training Naval aviators to fight against possible aerial foes.

*How do you get aerial photographs of a supersonic Talon when the camera platform is a Beech Bonanza capable of 190 mph max? The answer: with great difficulty! Skip Holm and Chuck Thornton managed to slow N638TC down with everything hanging out, giving a good idea of what the Talon looks like in landing configuration. The Talon pilot must be careful not to get the angle of attack (AOA) too high or the engines will flame out.*

Two years later, the aircraft went to the China Lake Naval Weapons center to become a drone, capable of being operated by radio control without a pilot aboard. During more than ten years at China Lake, this T–38 served as an air-to-air radar target, a chase plane, a pilot proficiency aircraft and in numerous other missions, both manned and unmanned. Unlike the vast majority of its fellow drones, which often served as missile targets, this

aircraft survived its service at China Lake—no mean feat!

In 1987, the trainer was transferred to NAS Fallon, Nevada, for use as a pilot proficiency aircraft. While it was being considered for permanent decommissioning and mounting on a pedestal at the base's entrance, NASA found out about the T–38. After careful inspection, NASA accepted the aircraft for service in the agency's T–38 fleet. After suitable modifications, the plane is now in service with NASA and will continue operating for many years.

With current USAF training requirements, the Talon will remain the Air Force's primary supersonic trainer until the year 2010. Over 62,000 pilots have trained in the Talon and the fleet has logged more than 10,000,000 flying hours.

The T–38 is also the USAF's safest supersonic aircraft. Despite the young trainees flying the type, the T–38's accident rate is half that for USAF fighters and attack aircraft.

At Sheppard AFB, Texas, T–38s continue to train pilots for twelve NATO nations. T–38s have also served for many years as chase planes for the recently retired SR–71 Blackbird, the Space Shuttle and, more recently, the Lockheed F–117A stealth fighter.

The 479th Tactical Fighter Training Wing at Holloman AFB, New Mexico, has employed modified T–38s for fighter lead-in training. Designated AT–38B, these Talons have been fitted with an SUU–11 7.62 mm mini-gun pod on the fuselage centerline. A total of 130 Talons were modified for this program.

Employed in many roles, worldwide, out of production since 1972 and with attrition reducing the number of flyable airframes, T–38s are not easily obtained for civilian use. But that didn't discourage one pilot.

Chuck Thornton had been bitten by the jet warbird bug during the 1970s when he was part owner of a civilian Sabre. After studying many types of jet aircraft, Thornton determined that the T–38 would be an ideal civilian machine since it had high performance and two seats. The Talon could be utilized for both test work and pleasure flying. However, there weren't any to be had!

Not one to easily give up, Thornton began to search out junkyards and was able to come up with a number of damaged airframes—aircraft that had been wrecked in USAF service, and once deemed economically unrebuildable, were stripped of useful parts and sold as scrap. By keeping a close eye on Department of Defense disposal sales, Thornton was able to acquire some new components to join his fleet of damaged Talons. Many of the parts were transported to Chino Airport and work on building a flying Talon began in the Unlimited Aircraft Ltd. facility. At first, the project appeared daunting to the casual observer, but Thornton was determined to have a flying Talon and he gathered a skilled crew of tech-

*Chuck Thornton and N683TC depart Van Nuys for another flight test mission. The beautifully finished "aggressor" Talon has just been joined by a second example, also built out of parts, and a Northrop F–5A Freedom Fighter that last saw service with the Royal Norwegian Air Force.*

nicians and mechanics who built a beautiful aircraft—better than anything the USAF had in service.

"Since I was starting from basically the ground up," states Thornton, "I was able to incorporate all the latest mods and add some features of my own." When completed, N638TC was a work of art and test flying showed all the skill, time and money invested in the plane had been worthwhile.

Thornton moved the Talon to Van Nuys, California, in 1984, once the airplane had been test flown and registered to FAA requirements. Maintained

in beautiful condition in a spacious hangar, Thornton also had a large parts inventory that was computer indexed, allowing the Talon to enjoy a high degree of readiness. Work for N638TC began to come in fast and furious. Northrop is a regular user of the plane for a number of their programs while the Talon has also been featured in national commercials and films. "When you own an expensive aircraft like the T-38A these various forms of employment go a long way to keeping the bird flying," says Thornton.

With N638TC being a business success, Thornton surveyed his stock of spares and decided it was time to build a second aircraft. As we go to press, his new Talon is complete and beginning flight testing. Thornton has also obtained a former Norwegian Air Force F-5A that will also be used on test programs. The Thornton hangar at Van Nuys is now home to three of Northrop's finest. And who knows what further Northrop jet warbirds he will add to his collection!

*Gold visor in place, Chuck Thornton awaits departure instructions from Van Nuys tower.*